UNSEEN BONDS

Lucas Fung

Copyright © 2026 Lucas Fung
ISBN: 978-1-923601-13-0

Published by Vivid Publishing
A division of Fontaine Publishing Group
P.O. Box 948, Fremantle
Western Australia 6959
www.vividpublishing.com.au

 A catalogue record for this book is available from the National Library of Australia

All rights reserved. No part of this publication may be reproduced, stored in a retrieval system or transmitted in any form or by any means, electronic, mechanical, photocopying, recording or otherwise, without the prior written permission of the copyright holder.

To my loving parents,
Thank you for supporting me.
Love, Lucas

Chapter One

◆

The "Perfect" Life

Samuel's pencil sliced across the page like a blade skimming over ice. It moved fast, precise, relentless, guided by a hand that seemed trained for perfection rather than expression. He did not simply write essays. He executed them. Each sentence landed with the clean finality of someone who believed mistakes were a personal weakness, each idea fitting into place as sharply as if carved from polished stone.

The maroon wooden desk beneath him creaked softly, its surface etched with decades of restless hands and bored scribbles left behind by students who had come and gone long before Samuel existed. Tiny grooves and faded initials covered every corner of it, except for one small square of polished space where Samuel worked. His desk was immaculate. His sphere. His sanctuary of order in a world that refused to offer any.

Every book aligned to the millimetre. Every sheet of paper unwrinkled and clean. His uniform, pressed until the fabric formed edges sharp enough to look dangerous under the fluorescent lighting, clung to him with rigid neatness. Even his hair, glossy and black, remained perfectly still, as though gravity itself respected the boundaries Samuel enforced upon his appearance.

Nothing dared fall out of place.

Not on his watch.

To anyone watching, Samuel Harper was exactly what he appeared to be. The kind of boy teachers admired. The kind parents used as examples. The kind other students whispered about when they thought he could not hear.

School Captain.

Captain of Academics.

Captain of Sports.

Captain of everything that could be measured, scored, or compared.

He was the boy who never failed.

He was the boy who could not fail.

Around him, the exam room crackled with tension. Pens scraped hurriedly against paper. Chairs twitched beneath fidgeting bodies. A few students tapped their feet so quickly the rhythm resembled hummingbird wings. Others sighed at intervals, as though their frustration could force the clock to move slower.

Samuel did not flinch. His breathing remained controlled, so quiet that the only sign he was alive came from the efficient movement of his hand. Yet if someone stared long enough, they would see the stiffness in his shoulders, the way tension coiled beneath his perfectly ironed shirt. That stiffness told a truth the rest of him tried to hide.

He risked a glance at the wall clock.

Thirty minutes left.

More than enough time for him.

Too much time for everyone else.

And far too much time for the pressure that pressed against his ribs like a familiar ache.

He had grown used to that ache. It had become a second heartbeat.

Ever since the divorce, since the house that echoed with emptiness rather than conversation, since the endless cycle of a father who tried too hard on some days and not at all on others, Samuel had learned to carry responsibility like armour. Perfection was his shield. His disguise. His protection.

If he was perfect, people left him alone.

If he was perfect, no one asked uncomfortable questions.

If he was perfect, the chaos stayed outside where it belonged.

He flexed his aching fingers, shook out his wrist, and read over his essay again. It was flawless. Coldly, harshly flawless. No edits needed. Perfection demanded nothing less, and Samuel delivered it without mercy.

He stood.

The sound of his chair scraping against the floor drew heads like a magnet. The soft murmurs started instantly, rippling through the students at the same time.

"He is done already?"

"Impossible."

"He is not real."

"How does he always finish first?"

The admiration and envy wove together, creating the same familiar background noise Samuel had lived with for years. He tried to ignore them, but their voices curled around him even as he walked.

He approached Mr Pine, essay pressed against his chest like a secret he refused to let others glimpse. Mr Pine looked up, eyebrows rising in mild surprise.

"Already done, Samuel?"

A single nod. Polite. Controlled.

Mr Pine smiled in that proud, approving way adults used when they believed they were witnessing promise. It should have felt warm. Encouraging. Instead it felt like another stone added to the growing weight Samuel carried.

Expectations. More of them. Always.

He turned away before the teacher could say anything else, pushing through the exam room door and stepping into the hallway. The moment it shut behind him, the world shifted.

Noise returned with startling force.

Gossip burst from clusters of students. Shoes struck the polished floors in uneven rhythms. A locker slammed so loudly it echoed down the corridor.

Someone behind him whispered with unnecessary clarity,

"Perfectionist."

Samuel's steps hesitated. The pause was so small it could have been overlooked. But inside him, the word landed with more force than he allowed anyone to see.

He kept walking.

Outside, the afternoon sun sprawled across the courtyard, spilling molten orange light over the school buildings. Clouds streaked the sky like brushstrokes. Laughter and chatter floated through the open space as students spilled across the grounds in disorderly clusters.

That joy stung Samuel's eyes more than the

sunlight did.

He walked faster, heading toward the gate with deliberate strides.

"HEY, SAMUEL!"

The shout exploded behind him, slicing through the air with a volume that made several students jump.

Samuel stiffened.

Theodore.

Tall. Athletic. Laughing even when no joke was told. His bright orange hair caught the sunlight like flames, making him look like he carried a little piece of summer everywhere he went.

He was everything Samuel was not.

"Hey, come watch my soccer game," Theodore said breathlessly as he jogged up beside him. "Or play. You run like you have engines in your legs. You would be amazing."

"No."

The word dropped between them with sharp finality.

Theodore blinked, caught off guard by the intensity of the answer. "You are sure? You never do anything after school."

Samuel did not reply. He could not explain the

tightness in his throat, the walls he had built, the rules he followed. Theodore sighed, raising a hand in a lazy, accepting gesture.

"Alright. Worth a try."

He turned back toward the oval, jogging away with his usual effortless energy.

Samuel took a single step forward.

Then he broke into a run.

Not the controlled stride he used in P.E.

A real run.

A desperate run.

He ran until his lungs burned.

He ran until the chatter behind him vanished.

He ran until the image of perfect, unbreakable Samuel fractured at the edges.

Sidewalks blurred. Cars honked. Someone shouted after him as he darted past with reckless speed. He did not slow down. He pushed harder, faster, as if he could outrun something clawing at his insides.

He ran until the scenery changed.

The old neighbourhood appeared like a forgotten memory.

Houses leaned slightly, as if tired of holding themselves up. Roof tiles sagged. Windows were clouded with age. Doors slanted on rusted hinges. Paint peeled away like weathered petals from fading flowers. Here, nothing was sharp or neat or perfect.

Here, the world was real.

Samuel slowed to a walk.

Then stopped in front of a small, crooked wooden house.

His home.

The door slid open with a long, aching groan. Darkness waited inside, soft and heavy. Samuel stepped in, his shoes landing on the familiar creaking boards.

No lights.

No footsteps.

No father.

Just the smell of dust, cool air, and something faintly metallic.

Samuel paused in the tiny entryway, letting his eyes adjust. His shoulders dropped almost imperceptibly, a tiny release that only someone who watched him closely would ever notice.

He whispered into the stillness,

"I am home."

His voice sounded too small for the empty room.

Too soft.

Like it belonged to a child who had forgotten how to speak loudly.

He set down his school bag and moved through the house as if walking through a memory. He opened his books. He lined up his pens. He prepared to work.

But the silence pressed against him.

Silence meant thinking.

Silence meant remembering.

Silence meant feeling.

And Samuel Harper avoided all three with the discipline of a soldier.

Because in the silence, sometimes he sensed something hollow inside him. Something that felt less like loneliness and more like absence. A missing piece. A shadow shaped almost like a person.

A half-remembered dream he never managed to grasp.

And with each passing day, that empty space inside him grew larger.

As if it were waiting for someone.

Or something.
He just did not know who.
Or why.
Not yet.

Chapter Two

♦

George's Struggle

The steady beeping of the heart monitor pulsed through the hospital room, a sound so constant that George should have stopped noticing it by now. But today, the rhythm felt louder than usual. It echoed inside his head, like footsteps drifting through a long and empty corridor.

Hospitals were supposed to be safe.
Clean.
Bright.
Filled with nurses who smiled and spoke gently.
But to George, they had always felt like cages.
White walls.
White sheets.

White lights.

Everything was too bright, too cold, too silent. The kind of silence that stripped away warmth, leaving nothing but a faint smell of disinfectant and air that tasted of loneliness.

George lay on his back, staring up at the ceiling tiles above him. Each one was the same size, the same colour, the same lifeless pattern. He could close his eyes and still see them. That was how long he had been here.

Time in the hospital did not flow normally.

Sometimes hours felt like days.

Sometimes days felt like nothing at all.

He tugged lightly at his faded blue hospital gown. The fabric brushed against his fingers, thin enough for light to pass through. Too thin. Too frail. Just like the way he felt inside these days.

A mixture of exhaustion and hopelessness pricked along his skin.

Then, a voice warmed the cold air.

"George, sweetheart?"

His mother's voice always came before he saw her.

Soft.

Warm.

Worried.

George turned his head. Sarah Miller stood in the doorway, framed by the white corridor light behind her.

She was the one constant in his fragile world.

Her once glossy hair was tied up in a loose ponytail, several strands escaping around her face. Dark shadows sat beneath her eyes, evidence of sleepless nights and too many fears carried alone. She held a tray with lunch on it, though George already knew he would not be able to eat more than a few bites.

Still, she smiled.

A tired smile.

But a real one.

"Mum," George whispered.

His voice was thin, like it might break apart if he spoke any louder.

Sarah set the tray down beside his bed. "I brought your favourite. Or at least what they think is your favourite here." She attempted a small laugh. "Hospital pasta will never be as good as the real thing."

George's lips twitched in a weak attempt at smiling. "It's fine," he whispered.

But even the smell of the food made his stomach curl.

Sarah noticed. She noticed everything.

Every flicker of discomfort.

Every forced smile.

Every bit of pain he tried to hide.

She sat on the edge of the bed and smoothed the blanket over his chest with slow, gentle movements. The same gesture she used when he was little and frightened by storms.

George swallowed. "Did the doctor come by?"

He already knew the answer. Doctors always came. They just did not always explain anything.

Right on cue, a soft knock sounded on the door.

Doctor Smith stepped inside.

Tall, kind-eyed, with a white coat that always smelled faintly of coffee and disinfectant. His glasses rested low on his nose, as though they, too, were tired.

He was the closest thing George had to comfort within these walls.

"Good afternoon, George," he said warmly.

George murmured, "You said good morning last time."

Doctor Smith blinked, then laughed lightly. "Did I?

My schedule must have swallowed half the day again."

George did not laugh, but the corner of his lips shifted slightly.

The doctor always treated him like a person, not a diagnosis on a chart.

Smith approached and opened the folder in his hands. "Just a routine check today. Nothing frightening."

George nodded, but his fingers curled around the blanket.

Routine meant needles.

Routine meant updates that rarely sounded hopeful.

Routine meant another day of waiting for a better that never seemed to arrive.

Doctor Smith adjusted the machines beside the bed, then checked George's blood pressure, heart rate, and temperature. His hands moved with a careful gentleness, as if touching something delicate enough to crack.

"You're looking stronger this week," the doctor said.

But George heard the hesitation behind the words.

So did Sarah.

Her hands tightened in her lap.

George closed his eyes.

He was tired.

Not the kind of tired that could be fixed by sleep.

The kind that lived deep in the bones.

The kind that came from fighting a battle every single day.

What hurt the most wasn't the pain.

It was the window.

Sometimes the world outside felt close enough to touch, and yet impossibly far away.

Today, faint laughter drifted in from the garden. Children his age were running on the grass, chasing balls, climbing trees. Their voices rose and fell with life.

Life he could not touch.

He turned his head toward the window. His reflection appeared faintly on the glass — pale cheeks, hollow eyes, thin arms that looked too fragile even for their own weight.

He looked nothing like the children outside.

He looked nothing like a normal twelve year old boy.

Doctor Smith's voice softened. "George? Are you

alright?"

George did not reply at first.

Then, so quietly that Sarah almost missed it, he whispered:

"I am tired, Doctor."

Not the kind of tired that meant wanting to nap.

The kind that meant he did not know how to keep living like this.

Doctor Smith's smile faltered.

He exchanged a glance with Sarah, a silent conversation full of fear and sympathy.

"We will take it one day at a time," the doctor said gently. "You are stronger than you believe."

George's throat tightened. His eyes stung.

"I do not feel strong."

Sarah immediately wrapped her arms around him. George leaned into her, resting his cheek against her shoulder. Her heartbeat trembled beneath his skin.

"Oh, sweetheart," she whispered. "I'm here. I'm always here."

Her voice shook.

For a few moments, he allowed himself to melt into her hold.

Not as a patient.

Not as a body strapped to machines.

Not as a problem waiting to be solved.

Just as a child who wanted to be normal.

After a while, Sarah brushed the hair away from his face. "George... do you want me to close the curtains? So you don't have to see outside?"

He hesitated.

A part of him wanted to shut out the world.

But another part needed to keep it in sight, to remember why he was still fighting.

"No," he whispered. "Let it stay open. It reminds me that I still want to get better."

Sarah blinked back tears.

Doctor Smith placed a steady hand on George's shoulder. "If you ever feel scared or sad... tell me. You don't need to pretend."

For the first time, George believed he meant every word.

Because today, something inside him was shifting.

A small spark flickered to life.

Hope.

A fragile, dangerous hope.

The kind that could hurt if it grew too bright.

The kind that came hand in hand with longing.

When the doctor left, the room returned to its quiet rhythm. The beeping of the machines continued their steady song.

George stared up at the ceiling.

He could not explain it, but something deep within him whispered:

Something is coming.

Something that will change everything.

His life — the quiet, lonely life locked behind hospital walls — was moving toward another life.

Someone out there shared a heartbeat that echoed faintly inside his own chest.

Someone he had never met, yet somehow recognised.

He did not know the truth yet.

But he felt it.

The world was shifting.

And his place in it was about to be rewritten.

Chapter Three

♦

The Family Secret

The late afternoon sun slanted through the small kitchen window, turning the floating dust into tiny specks of gold. A pot of soup simmered on the stove, sending out slow curls of steam that fogged the glass. It should have been a peaceful scene — warm, homey, ordinary.

But Jack Harper barely tasted any of it.

He stood at the counter, hand still wrapped around the wooden spoon he was using to stir the soup, though he hadn't moved it in nearly a minute. The broth had begun to bubble unevenly, a small island of foam forming in the centre.

He stared at it as if it could give him answers.

It didn't.

From the living room came the sound of soft laughter — not from the television, but the real, shrill, unrestrained laughter that only very young children could make. Two voices. Two boys. Twins.

Samuel and George.

Jack squeezed his eyes shut.

You'd think that a man with everything he'd once wanted — a home, a wife, two beautiful sons — would feel full. Complete.

Instead, his chest felt like it was being squeezed from the inside, his lungs never quite filling, his heart never quite able to settle into a normal rhythm.

"Jack? Dinner's almost ready?"

Sarah's voice floated in from the living room. Warm. Familiar. Tinged with something else he didn't like to name.

He cleared his throat and forced himself to move the spoon again. "Yeah. Nearly done," he called back, though his voice sounded flat even to his own ears.

He turned the heat down and wiped his hands on a tea towel, his movements automatic. He had done this a thousand times. It wasn't the soup that felt different tonight.

It was everything else.

He walked into the living room.

The space was small but cluttered with life, toy blocks scattered on the carpet, a painting one of the boys had done at preschool pinned crookedly to the wall, a half-built train track coiled under the coffee table like a sleeping snake.

On the worn sofa sat Sarah, her legs tucked under her, a stack of children's drawings on her lap. Her fingers smoothed absent-mindedly over a crayon scribble that might have been a dragon. Or a car. Or both.

She was smiling — sort of. It didn't quite reach her eyes.

Outside, through the thin curtains, the garden was drenched in sunlight. Two small figures darted across the patchy grass: identical in size, but not in movement.

Samuel ran in straight lines — sharp, determined, as if he were already racing towards some invisible finish line only he could see.

George moved in loops and pauses — stopping to crouch and examine a ladybird, then sprinting after his brother, then suddenly lying flat on the ground to stare up at the sky.

The sight twisted something inside Jack.

They're so small, he thought. So breakable.

And we've built this house on a fault line.

"Jack?" Sarah's voice brought him back. She had followed his gaze. Her fingers had stilled on the drawing. "You're miles away."

He sat down beside her, the sofa springs squeaking faintly. For a few seconds, they just watched the boys through the window.

Samuel pushed George lightly on the shoulder, pointing towards something only they could see. George laughed, eyes bright, and chased him.

"Remember when they couldn't even walk?" Sarah said, her voice suddenly soft. "You were terrified to leave them near the coffee table. You thought they'd just roll away."

Jack huffed a short, humourless laugh. "They almost did. Samuel rolled straight into the table leg. He glared at it like it did it on purpose."

"And George crawled over to pat him," she added, the ghost of a smile tugging at her lips. "He was always the gentler one."

A silence settled over them, heavy and fragile.

Jack swallowed. Now. You have to say it now.

"Sarah..." He didn't look at her. Couldn't. His fingers dug into his knees. "We need to talk."

Her body stiffened beside him. "That," she said quietly, "is never a good way to start a sentence."

He turned to face her.

There it was — the worry in her eyes, the tiredness in the lines around her mouth, the faint red along her lower eyelids that told him she hadn't been sleeping well.

He knew, in that moment, that she already knew.

"I don't think this is working," he forced out. "Us. The way we're living. The constant arguments, the money... the pressure. I don't know how much longer we can pretend everything's fine."

Sarah stared at the coffee table, at the chipped corner one of the boys had once banged into. "We're not pretending," she said softly. "We're... surviving."

"Barely." His voice came out sharper than he intended. "The bills are piling up. I'm working extra shifts, you're exhausted, the house—"

He broke off.

They both knew about the house — the constant dripping tap they never quite got around to fixing, the leaky roof, the windows that let in the cold wind in winter. The landlord's letter folded and refolded in the kitchen drawer.

"It's not just the house," he said more quietly. "It's us, Sarah. When was the last time we talked without snapping at each other? Really talked?"

Her hands tightened around the drawings.

"When was the last time we could?" she whispered. "Between your work, the boys' appointments, the late nights, the hospital..."

The word hung between them.

Hospital.

Just saying it made Jack's stomach twist.

George's first fainting episode.

The rushed ambulance ride.

The white corridors.

The doctor's serious expression.

They had stood together then. Held hands then. Cried together then.

But the stress hadn't left. It had only changed shape.

Sarah blinked rapidly, pulling herself back. She stared at her hands. "What are you saying, Jack?" she asked, though part of her clearly already knew.

He took a breath that felt like it burned all the way down.

"I'm saying..." He forced the words out. "We should consider a divorce."

The world seemed to hold its breath.

Outside, a bird chirped. A car drove past. The twins shrieked with laughter as one of them tripped and the other helped him up.

Inside, the room went very, very still.

Sarah didn't answer immediately. Her jaw worked. She looked at the window, at the boys, then at the floor.

When she finally spoke, her voice sounded as though it had been scraped raw.

"That's a big word to use between stirring soup and watching them play."

Jack winced. "I know. I'm sorry. I just— I don't know how else to say it."

"Try," she said.

He swallowed. His throat felt dry. "We're not... happy," he said. "Not really. We haven't been, for a long time. We argue about everything. Money. Schedules. The boys' future. The hospital bills. We're snapping at each other in front of them. That's not what I want them to learn about love."

Her shoulders slumped slightly.

"You think I want this?" Her voice trembled. "You think I don't lie awake every night wondering how I can fix it?"

The words pierced him.

"I know you try," he said quietly. "I do too. But trying isn't enough if it's hurting them."

A noise from outside drew their attention. George had fallen — not badly, just onto the grass. Samuel bent over, offering a hand. George took it.

They stood together, small and sturdy, side by side.

"They have each other," Jack said softly, half to himself. "They'll always have each other."

It struck him then like a lightning bolt — the thought that had been lurking in the shadows of his mind, hiding in all the cracks of his worry.

What if they don't?

He pushed that thought down quickly, but it left a residue.

Sarah followed his gaze. "I don't want them to grow up in a house full of anger," she whispered. "I don't want them to think staying in something broken is what you're supposed to do."

He looked at her properly then.

"You agree?"

She let out a long, shuddering breath. "I don't know what I agree with. I just know I'm tired. And I'm scared. And I don't want to lose them."

"You won't," he said instantly. "We won't take them from each other. They're... they're a pair. That's non-negotiable."

The conviction with which he said it surprised even himself.

"Twins," she murmured. "You can't split twins."

Her fingers drifted over the stack of drawings on her lap again, then she set them aside and reached for a nearby scrapbook.

It was a thick book, pages bulging slightly, the spine cracked from overuse. On the front, written in clumsy marker, were the words: "Samuel & George – Our Memories" — though the 'G' was backwards, from when Samuel had first tried to write it.

She opened it.

First tooth.

First steps.

First Christmas.

First day at childcare.

Two matching baby bibs. Two tiny hats. Two

sleeping infants in adjoining cots, fists loosely curled.

Sarah traced the photographs with the pad of her thumb.

"Look," she whispered. "They used to fit on one pillow. Both of them."

Jack leaned closer, the scent of old paper and glue filling his nose.

In one photo, Samuel and George sat in a bathtub, faces smeared with bubbles, Samuel reaching for the tap, George staring serenely at his brother.

In another, they lay on the grass as toddlers, holding onto the same teddy bear, each clutching one arm.

"How," Sarah said, her voice breaking, "are we supposed to tell them anything is changing at all?"

Jack didn't have an answer.

He watched a drop of something — water? soup? — fall from his hand onto the scrapbook page. Then realised it was neither.

He swiped at his eyes quickly. "Maybe we don't have to tell them yet," he said. "Not everything. Not...

all at once."

The moment he said it, a new unease stirred.

Secrets.

The house was already straining under the weight of unspoken things. Adding more felt like stacking teacups on a wobbly shelf.

But how could you explain something like divorce to two boys who still thought monsters lived in wardrobes?

Sarah closed the scrapbook carefully, as though it were something delicate that could break under too much pressure. "If we stay together," she said slowly, "we keep fighting in front of them. If we separate, we break their world in half."

"Either way, we hurt them," Jack said.

For a while, they sat in silence, the clock ticking loudly on the wall.

Tick.

Tick.

Tick.

Outside, the sun dipped a little lower.

Then, suddenly, the back door creaked open.

Samuel and George tumbled inside, cheeks flushed, hair windswept, the smell of grass clinging to their clothes.

"Mummy! Daddy! There was a beetle and it was THIS BIG!" George said, spreading his hands far wider than any beetle had a right to be.

"That's not how big it was," Samuel objected. "It was smaller. And you screamed."

"I did not scream."

"You did. You went 'AAAAAAAA—'"

"I was surprised," George corrected, chin jutting out.

Jack watched them, something inside him cracking a little more. They were so alive. So messy. So here.

Sarah forced a smile. "Alright, beast hunters. Upstairs. Baths, then pyjamas. Mummy and Daddy need to talk."

"Again?" Samuel complained. "You're always talking."

"That's what grown-ups do," Jack said weakly.

George paused on the first step, turning to look back at them. His grey eyes — softer than Samuel's sharper ones — lingered a moment too long.

"Mummy?" he asked suddenly. "Are you sad?"

The question hit Sarah like a gust of cold air.

She faltered. "Why would you say that, darling?"

He shrugged, small shoulders lifting. "Your face looks like when the doctor says 'I need to tell you something'."

Jack's heart missed a beat.

"Upstairs, George," Samuel muttered, tugging his brother's sleeve. "Mum's fine."

George hesitated, then nodded.

"Okay. Night, Daddy. Night, Mummy."

"Goodnight, love," Sarah whispered.

They listened to the boys' footsteps thudding up the stairs, then fading as a bedroom door clicked shut.

Jack exhaled slowly.

"I don't think we're hiding it as well as we think," he said.

"No," Sarah murmured. "I don't think we are."

She set the scrapbook down with trembling hands.

"Promise me something, Jack," she said, looking at him with an intensity that made him straighten.

"What?"

"Whatever happens between us," she said, "we don't let it destroy them. We don't let our choices be the reason they feel... abandoned. Or broken. We don't use them as pieces in a tug of war."

"We won't," he said. "I promise."

Something flickered in her eyes — relief, maybe. Or just exhaustion.

Then she added, in a voice so quiet he almost didn't hear it:

"And we don't keep them in the dark forever. Secrets have a way of... coming back."

He didn't understand, not fully.

Not yet.

But years later, when Samuel stood in a dimly lit office clutching a strange birth certificate, and George lay in a hospital bed asking questions Sarah could no longer avoid, those words would echo back through time.

For now, though, the only secret in the room was the one neither of them dared say aloud:

That somewhere, beneath the talk of bills and arguments and routines, they were both already wondering the same dangerous thing.

If we break this marriage to save ourselves...

how many pieces of our children's lives will fall with it?

Outside, in a small upstairs bedroom, two boys lay side by side in matching beds. Samuel stared at the ceiling, awake, sensing change without understanding it. George rolled closer, eyes half open.

"Do you think Mum's okay?" George whispered.

"She's fine," Samuel said automatically.

He didn't sound sure.

In the dark, George reached out and hooked his pinky finger around Samuel's.

Just in case.

Samuel didn't pull away.

Neither of them knew that in the years to come, that bond — that small, unconscious act of holding on — would be tested in ways none of them could imagine.

But for now, they slept.

And downstairs, their parents sat in a too-small living room, between soup that had gone cold and a scrapbook that felt suddenly heavier than paper ought to be, and decided — silently, separately — that something would have to change.

They just hadn't yet realised how much.

Or how many secrets would be born from that single, fragile decision.

Chapter Four

◆

Samuel's Curiosity

The kitchen was unusually quiet that evening. The hum of the refrigerator filled the silence with a faint vibration that Samuel had grown used to. It was the kind of sound that drifted into the background when the mind was busy, but tonight it pressed against him like a reminder of how empty the house felt.

He sat at the kitchen table with his homework spread neatly in front of him. The fading light from the sunset spilled across the floorboards, turning the wood into long tracks of gold. Outside, the neighbourhood children were still playing, their laughter echoing like distant bells. Samuel watched them through the window, wishing their joy did not sting as much as it did.

It was strange. He did not envy their games or their running or even their carefree spirits. What he envied was something harder to name. Something that felt like a memory without shape. A missing piece he could sense but not grasp.

His pencil hovered above the page but he could not focus. A faint pressure pushed at the back of his mind, like the whisper of a forgotten dream. He tried to remember the strange dream he had the night before, the dream where he had seen another boy standing in a world made of ripples and clouds. A boy who felt familiar. Too familiar.

Who was he?

Samuel pressed a hand to his forehead. The ache had started again, a dull throb that came whenever he tried to remember things that did not quite exist.

Later that evening he wandered toward his father's office. The door was slightly open, warm yellow light spilling from the crack. He heard Jack's voice inside. Tired. Strained. Filled with something heavy.

He slowed his steps.

"I do not know if he is ready," Jack said. His voice sounded as if it had travelled a long distance before reaching the room. "What if he finds out on his own. I cannot bear what that might do to him."

There was a pause. Samuel held his breath. No other voice answered, which meant Jack was on the phone. He seemed unaware of how thin the walls in the house were.

Something is wrong.

Samuel stepped back before he could be caught listening. His heartbeat thudded in his chest. His father's tone was not angry. It was fearful. And fear from a parent was always the kind that meant truth was hiding in the shadows.

That night, sleep came slowly.

The moon cast pale light onto Samuel's bedroom walls as he lay in bed with his eyes open. He tried to force himself to be still, but the restlessness inside him grew stronger. The dream from the night before hovered at the edge of his memory. The boy in the grey world. His eyes. The way Samuel had felt a connection that made no sense.

He whispered into the quiet room.

"Who are you?"

His voice disappeared into the darkness.

When he woke the next morning he felt a tugging sensation. It pulled him through the hallway like an invisible thread guiding him to his father's office. Jack had already left for work. The house felt empty and the silence gave Samuel courage he did not have the night before.

He pushed the office door open fully.

Piles of paper were scattered across the desk, but one folder stood out. A thick folder with a label written in small faded letters that caught the light.

Family Records.

The world shifted.

His pulse quickened as he stepped closer. His hand trembled slightly when he touched the folder. For a moment he hesitated, wondering whether this counted as betrayal. Then he remembered the tired voice from the night before. And the dream. And the ache inside him.

He opened the folder.

The papers inside smelled of old air and dust. Hospital documents. Notes in his father's handwriting. Certificates. Dates.

Then he saw it.

A document with his own full name printed at the top. His breath caught. He scanned it from top to bottom until something jumped out at him.

Under the word Birth Information there was a faint line that made his blood freeze.

Twin brother.

Name not recorded.

A hollow emptiness opened inside him.

Twin.

He had a twin.

No one had ever told him.

His hands began to shake. He read the line again. And again. Suddenly the dream made sense. The strange echoing feeling that had followed him for years made sense. The ache, the emptiness, the sense of someone missing. All of it.

Why had they hidden this from him?

A floorboard creaked from the hallway.

Samuel jumped, quickly closing the folder and placing it back exactly where it had been. His heart hammered in his chest. He forced his breathing to slow down as footsteps approached the kitchen. It was only the neighbour's cat slipping through the open window, brushing against a chair and startling itself.

Samuel pressed a hand to his chest, trying to calm the panic.

Later that day his father returned from work. Samuel watched him with new eyes as Jack prepared dinner. Every movement suddenly looked heavy, as if he carried invisible bags filled with secrets.

They ate quietly, the clinking of cutlery the only

sound.

Samuel kept looking at Jack, searching his face. Jack noticed.

"You seem quiet, Sam. Everything alright?" he asked gently.

Samuel forced a nod. "Just tired."

Jack reached out and ruffled Samuel's hair. The touch had always felt comforting. Today it felt like the hand of someone hiding a truth too large to speak.

Samuel wanted to ask. He wanted to say the words that were pounding inside him.

Do I have a brother?

Why did you hide it?

Who is he?

Where is he?

But the look of exhaustion in Jack's eyes stopped him. The questions lodged in his throat like stones.

That night he lay in bed again, staring at the ceiling. The moonlight flowed in through the window, casting a pale glow across his blanket.

He whispered the truth to himself, the truth he could no longer deny.

"I am not alone."

The ache inside him shifted. It no longer felt like

emptiness. Now it felt like a beginning.

A beginning that frightened him.

But also a beginning that he needed.

Somewhere out there was someone whose life was tied to his. Someone whose presence he had once felt in dreams. Someone whose absence had shaped every quiet moment of his childhood.

He pulled the blanket tighter around himself and shut his eyes.

Tomorrow, he promised silently.

Tomorrow, I will find the truth.

Even if it changes everything.

Chapter Five

♦

George's Resilience

George had been awake since dawn, though he was too tired to lift his head from the pillow. Morning light seeped through the thin white curtains, turning the hospital room a soft shade of gold. The light was gentle but even that felt like too much today. His body ached in quiet ways that were difficult to describe, a kind of heaviness that lived in every breath and every blink.

Despite everything, he forced himself to sit up.

He always tried to sit up. It was his way of fighting back.

The room around him was unchanged. The same white walls. The same faint scent of disinfectant that clung to the air. The same silence broken only by steady beeps from the monitor beside his bed.

He had memorised the sounds by now. He knew which beep meant everything was fine, which beep meant a nurse would check on him soon, and which beep meant someone had accidentally pulled on a wire again.

He wished he could forget the sounds. But forgetting was impossible here.

His mother entered the room quietly, carrying a

small tray with breakfast. Her steps were soft, as though any loud noise might make him break into pieces. She always tried to look cheerful in the morning but today the worry in her eyes was harder to hide.

"Good morning, love," she said as she set the tray onto the table beside him.

George managed a small greeting. "Morning, Mum."

His voice was thin. He hated when it sounded so small.

Sarah sat on the edge of the bed and brushed a hand through his hair. Her fingers were warm, which made the cold inside him feel less sharp. "Did you sleep well?" she asked gently.

"Not really," he admitted.

Sarah's expression tightened for a moment, then softened again. "I thought so. You had a rough day yesterday."

George stared at the breakfast on the tray. Toast. A cup of milk. A bit of fruit. He knew he had to eat, but today the thought made his stomach twist. The sight of the food felt too heavy, like it belonged to someone else.

A knock on the door broke the silence.

Doctor Smith stepped in, holding a folder in one hand. His face carried the calm confidence that George found strangely reassuring. He always seemed to bring a small bit of sunlight into the room with him, even on the worst days.

"Good morning, George," he said warmly. "How are we feeling today?"

George gave a weak shrug. "Still here."

Doctor Smith chuckled softly. "That is already something to be proud of."

The doctor pulled up a chair and sat beside the bed. "We will do a few simple checks today. No surprises."

That was supposed to comfort him.

It did not.

He watched as Doctor Smith checked his pulse and examined the chart on the monitor. The doctor's face remained calm but George had become very good at reading the things adults tried to hide. There was a tiny crease between Doctor Smith's eyebrows. A pause that lasted a moment too long.

George looked away, pretending not to notice.

After the routine checks were done, the doctor placed the stethoscope back around his neck. "You have been very brave," he said with a gentle smile. "You are doing your best. That matters more than anything."

George stared at his hands. His fingers were thin and pale. "I do not feel brave," he said quietly.

Doctor Smith leaned in slightly. "Bravery does not mean you are not scared. It means you keep going even when everything feels hard. And you do that every single day."

The room fell silent for a moment.

A burst of laughter from outside came through the slightly open window. Children playing in the hospital garden. The sound drifted into the room like sunlight riding on air.

George lifted his head, listening.

He could almost picture them. Running. Jumping.

Throwing a ball. Breathing in fresh air without a machine watching their every move.

His heart tightened with longing.

He wanted to be out there. Even five minutes would have been enough. Five minutes to run without feeling dizzy. Five minutes where his body did not remind him of its limits.

Sarah saw the expression on his face and her eyes softened. She stood up and closed the curtains slowly. "Maybe it is better if we do not look outside right now."

George hesitated before responding.

"No," he whispered. "I want to see it. I want to remember what normal feels like."

His mother paused, then nodded and reopened the curtains. Sunlight poured in. The children outside continued their games, unaware of the boy watching them from a window that might as well have been a wall of glass.

A memory rose unexpectedly in George's mind. A moment from long ago. He had been younger then, maybe four or five. He remembered playing in a backyard that smelled like summer. Someone had been with him. A child with dark hair and quick steps. A child who ran ahead and kept turning back as if to make sure George was still following.

He blinked hard.

Who was that boy?

Sarah noticed the sudden shift in his expression. "Sweetheart? Are you alright?"

George opened his mouth then closed it again. The memory drifted away like fog dispersing in warm air. He could not catch it.

"I am fine," he said softly. "Just thinking."

Sarah did not press further. She knew forcing answers never helped.

A little later, when the doctor had left and the breakfast tray had been removed, George leaned back onto the pillow and closed his eyes. The quiet hum of the machines filled his ears. The room felt colder than before.

"Mum," he said suddenly.

"Yes, love?"

He hesitated.

His voice trembled slightly. "Do you think I will get better?"

Sarah froze, just for a heartbeat. Then she forced a reassuring smile to her face, although her eyes shone with a sadness that no child should ever have to see.

"Of course you will," she whispered, taking his hand. "You are strong. Stronger than you believe."

George squeezed her hand back.

"I am trying," he whispered.

"I know," she breathed.

She kissed his forehead, then pulled the blanket up a little higher.

After she left for a moment to speak with a nurse outside, George stared up at the ceiling and let the silence wrap around him. He felt something new today. A quiet determination hidden beneath the fear. A spark.

If he could not run outside like the children in the garden, he would still find a way to move forward. Even if the steps were small. Even if the world kept shrinking into this room.

He imagined one day walking out of the hospital. Feeling the wind on his face. Meeting someone who felt strangely familiar. Someone whose absence felt like a shadow that had followed him his whole life.

He did not understand the feeling completely, but it made his heart beat faster.

Hope was frightening.

But it was also alive.

And George held onto it the way a drowning person holds onto the surface of the water.

Quietly. Desperately.

With everything he had.

Chapter Six

◆

The Dream

George did not remember falling asleep. One moment he was staring at the ceiling of his hospital room, feeling the weight of exhaustion pressing against his ribs. The next moment he was standing in a place that did not belong to the world he knew.

A grey sky stretched endlessly above him, pale and soft like brushed silk. The entire horizon glowed with a gentle silver light, as if dawn had been paused in the middle of rising. Beneath his feet was something that looked like water yet behaved like solid ground. When he shifted his weight, ripples shimmered from his shoes, dancing outwards in perfect circles.

He took a breath.

The air tasted clean. Too clean. As if every scent had been washed away and replaced with something pure and unfamiliar.

Where am I?

He took a step forward. The surface beneath him rippled again but did not sink. It felt like walking on a dream made real.

His body felt different here. Light. As if the heaviness of illness had been left somewhere far behind. His lungs expanded easily, without the usual ache. His head felt clear. It was the kind of freedom he had forgotten could exist.

He closed his eyes, letting the breeze sweep across his face. A warmth spread through his chest. Peace. Real peace.

Then he heard it.

A soft breath.

A sound that did not belong to him.

He opened his eyes.

Someone was lying a short distance away, face pressed against the mirrored ground. A boy. George froze.

The boy lifted his head.

George felt his heart lurch.

It was the boy from his dream before.

Or from the memory.

Or from the place inside his mind he never quite understood.

Dark hair.

Clear eyes.

A face so familiar that George felt a strange tug inside his chest, the same kind of feeling that came from a memory too old to recall clearly yet too important to forget.

The boy sat up quickly, startled. He scrambled back a little, eyes wide. George mirrored him without meaning to, both of them reacting like reflections.

For a brief moment, neither spoke.

Not because they did not want to.

But because something in this place had no room for spoken words.

George tried to greet him. His lips moved. No sound came out.

The boy frowned in confusion and tried to speak too. Nothing.

They looked at each other with the same bewilderment.

George raised a hand to wave. The boy raised his

own at the exact same time. George blinked. That was not just imitation. It felt almost like... instinct.

The boy leaned forward, studying him closely. His eyes focused on George's left eye. George, in turn, noticed a faint glimmer in the boy's right eye, almost like a tiny light pulsing beneath the surface. He wondered if the boy saw the same glow in him.

The air around them shifted.

Something invisible connected them.

Not a string.

Not a rope.

Something more delicate.

Something more ancient.

A shared beat of the heart.

A shared breath.

A shared existence.

George's chest tightened with a sudden rush of emotion. He did not understand it but he felt it.

This boy was not a stranger.

The clouds above parted slightly, revealing a sliver of brightness that scattered soft light across their faces. Time seemed to slow, as if the grey world was waiting for something.

The boy took a hesitant step forward.

George did the same.

Then, without warning, something inside George pulled sharply. His vision blurred. The world trembled.

He staggered.

His hands began to fade, becoming see through like smoke dissolving into the air. Panic surged through him. He looked at the boy with wide eyes and pointed frantically to his fading arms.

The boy's face filled with alarm.

He reached out his hand.

His movements became frantic, filled with desperation.

George wanted to reach back.

He wanted to touch the boy's hand.

He wanted to stay.

But the pull was too strong.

His body continued to fade. His legs disappeared first. His chest next. His arms turned into wisps of pale light.

The boy tried to run to him but the distance between them stretched the more he moved. It was as if the dream itself refused to let them meet.

George watched him with a heart full of longing and fear.

He wanted to say something.

Anything.

Wait.

Do not go.

Do not forget me.

But no sound came.

In the last moment before he completely vanished, he saw the boy fall to his knees, reaching out with trembling fingers, eyes full of a sadness that tore through

George like lightning.

Then everything dissolved.

Darkness swept through him, swallowing him whole.

At the very same moment, Samuel woke in his bed with a gasp, sheets tangled around him, his heart pounding like a drum inside his chest. Sweat clung to his forehead even though the room was cold.

He pressed both hands to his chest.

The feeling of the dream had not left him. It clung to him like warmth from a fire he had been too close to. His hands still tingled where he had tried to reach for the fading boy.

He shut his eyes tightly and whispered into the quiet air of his room.

"You are real."

He did not know why he felt so certain.

He did not understand the connection.

But the truth glowed inside him with a certainty stronger than anything he had ever known.

Somewhere out there

in a world far beyond his walls
someone was waiting for him.
Someone who felt like part of him.
Someone who was missing.

He sat up slowly, breathing through the aftershocks of the dream.

Tomorrow
he told himself again
Tomorrow I will find you.

Chapter Seven

♦

The Search Begins

Samuel woke before the sun rose.

The sky outside his window was still dark, lined with faint streaks of silver where the dawn waited to break. His room felt colder than usual, and the air carried a strange heaviness, as though the dream from the night before was still lingering somewhere unseen.

He sat up and rubbed his eyes. His breaths came out uneven, the same quiet tremors that always followed the dream. Except this time the feeling did not fade. It stayed with him, pulsing gently beneath his ribs.

He pushed aside his blankets and placed his feet on the floor. The moment he stood, he felt it again. A tug. A pull. Something inside him whispering that he needed to move. That staying still was no longer possible.

He walked to the mirror beside his desk.

His reflection stared back

pale skin

dark hair slightly messy

eyes still clouded with sleep and confusion.

For a moment he imagined the other boy standing beside him, faint like a ghost from memory. He imagined the boy breathing the same air, sharing the same heartbeat, looking into the same mirror with the same question.

Who are you to me?

Samuel closed his eyes and whispered into the reflection.

"I will find you."

He did not know how.

He did not know where to start.

But he knew he had to try.

He dressed quickly and walked to the kitchen.

The house was silent.

Jack had not woken yet.

The floorboards creaked under Samuel's feet as he moved past the dining table and into the hallway.

His father's office door was closed.

He paused in front of it, his hand hovering near the doorknob. The memory of yesterday returned with sharp clarity. The folder labelled Family Records. The document with the words that had changed everything.

Twin brother.

Name not recorded.

His heartbeat thudded beneath his ribs.

A cold wave swept through him.

He knew he should not enter without permission.

He knew it was wrong.

Yet something deeper urged him forward.

He opened the door slowly.

The faint smell of old paper filled the room. Jack's desk lamp, still left on from the night before, cast a warm glow over the papers. The folder sat in the exact same place.

Samuel approached with careful steps.

His hands trembled slightly as he reached for it.

He opened the folder.

The document was still there.

The words still burned into the page.

Twin brother.

Name not recorded.

He read it again and again, hoping the paper might suddenly give him more answers. It did not. It held its silence with a kind of cold patience.

There was another sheet beneath it.

He lifted it.

This one was older

the edges yellowed

the ink slightly faded.

It appeared to be a hospital record, but several lines had been covered with a dark marker. Someone had tried to hide something.

Why?

Why erase information?

What was so dangerous that it had to be blacked out?

He flipped through the pages until he reached the last one. A small slip of paper fell out. Samuel bent down and picked it up.

It was a postcard.

A simple postcard with a faded photograph of a small seaside town. There was no writing on the back except a date that had been faintly stamped in purple ink.

Twelve years ago.

The year he was born.

His breath caught.

He studied the postcard closely. The town looked unfamiliar yet strangely important, as if his heart recognised it even though his mind did not.

He slipped the postcard into his pocket.

Just then, he heard footsteps approaching from the hallway.

He froze.

Jack's voice followed.

"Sam, you awake?"

Samuel quickly placed the papers back exactly as they were. He closed the folder, stepped away from the desk, and pretended he had just passed by the room.

Jack appeared at the doorway, rubbing his eyes. "You are up early," he murmured.

Samuel forced a calm expression. "Could not sleep."

His father nodded slowly, not questioning it. "Breakfast soon. I will make something."

Samuel hesitated. "Can I walk to school on my own today?"

Jack stopped.

He looked at Samuel with a mixture of surprise and

caution. "On your own? That is quite a distance."

"I want to think," Samuel said quietly. "Just for a bit."

Jack studied him for a moment, then nodded. "Alright. But stay safe. And send me a message when you arrive."

"I will."

Samuel stepped outside.

The air was crisp and cool.

The sky was beginning to brighten.

Birds chirped from the rooftops.

He clutched the postcard in his pocket and began walking.

Each step felt heavy

but the heaviness came with purpose.

As he walked through the quiet streets

past familiar houses and morning lights

his mind kept returning to the dream.

The boy's face

the desperation in his eyes

the way the dream pulled them apart

the sense of loss that clung to Samuel like smoke.

He knew the dream was not just a dream.

He knew the connection was more than imagination.

The truth was buried somewhere.
Hidden under secrets.
Hidden behind blacked out lines.
Hidden in the missing name.
And now that he knew, he could not stop.
Not until he found him.

He reached a small park on the way to school. Children would come here later in the day but for now it was empty. The swings creaked softly in the morning breeze.

Samuel sat on one of them.
He took out the postcard.
The seaside town looked peaceful.
Quiet streets
blue water
small houses near the shore
and a lighthouse standing proudly on a rocky hill.
Why did his father keep this?
Why was it in the folder?
What did this place have to do with him
with his twin

with everything that had been hidden?

He turned the card in his hands.

The date on the back shimmered faintly in the sunlight.

The year of his birth.

His fingers tightened around the edge.

He whispered a promise to the empty park.

"I will find the truth."

At that same moment

in the hospital

George sat up in bed, eyes wide.

His heart suddenly raced

as if someone far away had called out to him

with a voice he somehow recognised.

He pressed a hand to his chest, confused.

Why did it feel like someone was looking for him?

The dream returned in a rush

the boy reaching out

the panic

the fading light.

He whispered into the quiet room.

"Come back."

Neither boy knew that their paths

though separated by distance and secrets

had already begun to move toward each other.
The search had begun.
And the world they knew
was already changing.

Chapter Eight

♦

George's Hope

The hospital room felt quieter than usual.
Too quiet.

George sat propped up against the pillows, knees slightly bent under the thin blanket. Outside, the sky was pale, brushed with soft morning light that filtered through the window and rested on the edge of his bed. The light made the room look gentler than it really was.

He stared at his hands.

They were thinner than he remembered from a year ago. Bones more visible. Skin more fragile. When he flexed his fingers, he could feel the slight tremble that came when his body was too tired.

A nurse had taken his blood earlier that morning.

Another test. Another result that would be whispered about in hallways, then translated for his mother in careful, gentle words.

He was used to it.

But today, for some reason, the usual routine felt different.

As if something was waiting just outside the door.

As if the world was holding its breath.

The door opened with a soft click.

Sarah stepped in, carrying a plastic cup of juice and a small plate with biscuits. Her hair was tied back in a ponytail that had begun to loosen, a few strands falling over her face. Her smile appeared on cue, but her eyes were too bright.

"Here you go, love," she said, placing the cup on the bedside table. "Orange juice. Not as good as the fresh one at home, but still something."

George watched her.

"Mum," he said quietly. "You look tired."

She blinked, surprised. "Do I?"

He gave a tiny nod.

She tried to shrug it off with a laugh. "That is what happens when your son keeps making me worry."

He smiled faintly, but the smile did not last.

"Did the doctor say anything new?" he asked.

The question made her pause for a fraction of a second.

A fraction, but George saw it.

She sat down on the chair beside his bed, folding her hands in her lap. "They are still going through the tests," she replied. "Doctor Smith says they want to keep an eye on you a little longer. Just to make sure everything is stable."

George looked at the heart monitor. The line pulsed in steady little hills.

Stable.

That word had begun to feel like a cage.

His gaze drifted to the window. Children were playing on the hospital lawn again. Not many, just a few. A girl with a bright pink jacket chased a boy with a paper plane. Their voices floated up to the window, light and full of life.

He watched them as if watching another world.

"Mum," he said suddenly, eyes still on the children. "Do you ever feel like there is something you are not telling me?"

The room turned still.

Sarah's fingers tightened around each other. "What makes you ask that?" she replied softly.

George took a breath. "I do not know. Sometimes I feel like there is a piece of my life missing. Something that should be there but is not. I feel it when I look outside. Or when I dream. Or when..." He hesitated. "Or when you look at me like I am about to disappear."

Her eyes filled with tears.

She looked away, toward the window, as if searching for the right words in the shifting light.

"You are not going to disappear," she whispered. "You are here. That is all that matters."

He turned his head to look at her properly. "Then why do you always look sad when you think I am not watching?"

The question cut through the air like a thin blade.

Sarah let out a breath that seemed to leave with more weight than it arrived. She stood up and began to straighten items that did not need straightening. The pillow. The corner of the blanket. The small plastic cup.

"George," she began, "there are things that are hard for adults to talk about. Not because they want to lie.

But because they are afraid of what the truth might do."

He watched her, silent.

She turned back to him. "When you were younger," she said slowly, "your father and I made some choices. We thought we were doing what was best. For us. For you." Her voice trembled. "I am starting to realise that some of those choices might have hurt you. Even if you did not know it."

George's heart began to race.

"This is about him, isn't it?" he asked.

She frowned. "About who?"

"My father," George said. "Properly. Not the parts you tell me in small pieces. The whole story. About why he is not here. About why he and you look like you are always carrying something too heavy."

Sarah stared at him.

For a long moment, she did not move.

Then she sat back down, her shoulders sinking. "You are too clever," she murmured. "You see too much."

He waited.

She folded her hands together again. "Your father and I were different people back then," she said. "We were young. We had dreams. We thought love would be enough to fix everything. But life was complicated. There was money. There were arguments. There was stress from work. We tried to stay together for as long as we could."

Her eyes glistened.

"And then there was you. And your brother."

George froze.

The word hit him like a shock.

"Brother," he repeated, almost in a whisper.

His mind flashed to the dream.

To the boy in the grey sky.

To the boy whose eyes had felt like a missing echo of his own.

Sarah closed her eyes.

She had not meant to say it so suddenly. The word slipped out because she was tired. Tired of carrying it alone. Tired of burying truth under thick layers of silence.

George's voice shook. "I have a brother."

She nodded slowly.

"Why," he asked, the question pressing against his ribs, "have you never told me?"

Her hands trembled where they lay in her lap. "I thought it would protect you," she whispered. "I thought if you did not know what you had lost, it would hurt less."

He stared at her, unable to speak.

Lost.

The word rang inside his head.

"What happened to him?" he forced out. "Where is he?"

She swallowed hard. "He is with your father."

The world tilted.

"So you split us," George said quietly. "You kept me. He took him."

Tears finally rolled down Sarah's cheeks. She did not bother to wipe them away. "I fought," she said. "We argued. We shouted. We said things we did not mean. Your father wanted to take you both. I wanted to keep you both. In the end, the only thing we could agree on was something horrible. We each took one child. We told ourselves it was temporary. That one day we would fix it. Bring you back together."

She shook her head.

"Time passed. The anger stayed. The guilt grew. The distance between us became wider and wider. And you kept getting sicker. I could not bear to add more questions to your life when you already had so many."

George listened in silence.

He thought about all the nights he had laid awake feeling something missing without knowing what it was. All the times he had stared out of windows, sensing someone out there he was meant to meet. All the moments in dreams when he had seen a figure that felt like a mirror.

He had not been imagining it.

It had been real all along.

"What is his name?" George asked, voice barely audible.

She hesitated.

Just for a moment.

"Samuel," she whispered. "Your twin brother is named Samuel."

The name poured through him like warmth and ice at the same time.

He whispered it again, tasting the shape of it. "Samuel."

His chest ached.

"How could you keep him from me?" he asked, his voice trembling. "How could you let us grow up without knowing each other existed?"

Sarah covered her face with her hands. "Because I was afraid," she said. "Afraid that if you knew, you would hate me. Afraid you would ask to leave. Afraid you would choose him and your father and I would lose you completely. So I did the worst thing. I tried to pretend the missing half did not exist."

George felt tears burning behind his eyes.

He blinked them away.

"Mum," he said slowly, his voice steadier now. "I do

not hate you. But I need to know him. I need to know who my brother is. I need to know why I feel like part of me is out there, living a life I have never seen."

She dropped her hands and looked at him.

In his face she saw the small boy he once was, clutching her hand in hospital waiting rooms. She saw his first fever. His first scared question. His first brave smile. She also saw the part of him that was not only hers. The part that belonged to another child, somewhere else, carrying the same history without knowing it.

"I do not know if your father is ready," she said. "He has his own guilt. His own secrets. I do not know what he has told Samuel. He might not even have told him about you."

"Then it is time he does," George answered.

His voice surprised even himself.

It sounded older.

Stronger.

"I want to meet him," he said. "Even if it is only once. Even if I am still sick. Even if it is hard. I want to see him with my own eyes. I want to hear his voice. I want to know if he has the same dreams."

The door opened.

Jack stood there.

He looked older than in George's memories. His hair had more grey at the temples. His shoulders carried an invisible weight. His eyes moved from Sarah to George, sensing at once that something important had just been spoken.

For a moment the three of them simply looked at each other.

Sarah rose to her feet. "Jack," she said quietly. "He knows."

George met Jack's gaze.

"You have a brother," Jack said at last, his voice rough. "And his name is Samuel. I should have told you years ago."

George took a breath that felt like crossing a line he could never return from.

"Then help me find him," he said.

Jack hesitated. Guilt and fear flickered across his face. Then something else appeared. The faintest trace of hope.

He nodded.

"We will tell you everything," he said. "No more secrets."

Outside the window

the children continued to play on the lawn

their laughter drifting upward.

Inside the room

George felt something shift inside his chest.

For the first time in a long time

his hope did not feel like a distant light he could never reach.

It felt closer.

It had a name.

It had a face from his dreams.

Samuel.

Somewhere out there

his brother existed.

And now that he knew

George refused to let the truth disappear again.

Chapter Nine

◆

Sarah's Confession

Night drifted slowly over the city, settling like a deep velvet curtain drawn gently across the sky. One by one, the streetlights flickered on in the quiet dusk, their pale halos stretching over the damp pavement. The world seemed to exhale as the day folded into darkness.

Samuel sat at his desk, unmoving, the tip of his pencil hovering above the page. His exercise book lay neatly open, every line of handwriting sharp, controlled, and perfectly aligned. Yet his mind had abandoned every word. The quiet of the room pressed against his ears.

The ticking of the wall clock sounded louder than usual.

Clear.

Precise.

Relentless.

Each second landed with a small echo inside his ribs, as if time itself was tapping gently, checking whether he was still listening.

He lifted his head and gazed toward the window.

Outside, the evening had deepened into a soft blue shadow. Trees stood like silhouettes, their leaves whispering as a light wind brushed past. Traffic hummed faintly in the distance, rising and falling like waves. The city was settling into its nightly rhythm.

A thin shiver ran down Samuel's spine.

Not because the room was cold, but because something inside him felt unsettled, as if a quiet pull had begun deep in his chest. It was soft at first, like the brush of a feather, yet persistent. It tugged again, steady and rhythmic. He pressed a hand to the center of his chest.

His heart was beating strangely.

Not fast.

Not weak.

Just... different.

He closed his eyes and breathed in slowly.

And the dream returned.

That dream.

The place washed in grey light, quiet like a world between worlds.

A boy standing across from him.

A boy who looked at him with eyes full of longing, surprise, and something Samuel could only describe as recognition.

The boy's hand reaching toward him.

Samuel reaching back.

The world dissolving before their fingers touched.

He opened his eyes sharply. His breath caught in his throat.

That dream did not feel like a dream.

It felt like a memory, misplaced yet deeply familiar.

Wind brushed against the windowpane, making a soft tapping sound. Samuel stood abruptly, feeling the same internal tug grow stronger. He walked to the window, fingertips grazing the cold glass.

Outside, the moon sat low, half-covered by drifting clouds.

Its light was faint, but enough to draw out the

contours of the rooftops and the slight shine of leaves swaying in the night air.

Samuel pressed his forehead lightly against the glass.

He should have felt alone.

That was the normal feeling at this hour.

But tonight, the silence did not feel empty.

It felt full.

Filled with a presence he could not see.

The strange heartbeat fluttered again in his chest, and for a moment he felt as if it was not his own heartbeat at all. As if someone else's rhythm was blending with his.

He whispered, barely audible, "Who are you."

His breath fogged a small patch of the glass. The words dissolved into the quiet room, unanswered.

He stepped back from the window and turned to his desk, where the postcard lay waiting. The faded photograph of the seaside town shimmered faintly in the slant of moonlight that filtered through the curtain. The lighthouse in the picture stood tall, its painted beam of light frozen mid sweep.

Samuel reached for it slowly.

The moment his fingers touched the edge, his

heartbeat jumped again.

A pulse.

A call.

A response.

He pressed the postcard to his chest.

The night deepened, the shadows growing long and still.

His shoulders tensed as a sudden certainty washed over him.

Someone out there was feeling the same pull.

Someone was awake at this hour, breathing through the same strangeness, sensing the same invisible thread winding slowly between their hearts.

Somewhere far away, in a quiet hospital room.

George's eyes snapped open.

Darkness surrounded him, soft and unmoving. The machines beside his bed blinked calmly, their small lights reflecting off the metal rails. The faint click of the IV pump sounded like a heartbeat in the silence.

His mother was asleep in the chair next to him, her hand resting lightly over his forearm. Her breathing was steady, slow and peaceful in a way he rarely saw during the day.

George lay still, afraid to disturb her.

Yet something inside him was stirring.

His heart.

Beating faster.

Stronger.

With a new rhythm that felt impossibly familiar.

The sensation rose in him like a tide, slow but unstoppable. He pressed his other hand to his chest.

It was back.

The strange pulse.

The one that did not belong to him alone.

He looked toward the window.

Moonlight flowed into the room in a gentle beam, casting a pale glow across the floor. It made the room look different. Softer. Fuller. The light brushed the edge of George's bed like a hand reaching for him.

His eyes filled with emotion he could not name.

The feeling inside him was not fear.

Not illness.

Not the tightness that came before a painful night.

It was something else entirely.

Someone out there was awake.

Someone whose heartbeat he could sense as clearly as his own.

Someone his soul seemed to recognise even though

his mind did not.

His voice trembled as he whispered into the moonlit darkness, "Who are you."

His mother stirred slightly but did not wake.

George kept staring at the window, his fingers trembling around the blanket.

The pulse in his chest grew stronger.

A steady, shared rhythm.

As though two hearts separated by distance were beginning to align.

He did not understand it, yet he felt it deeply.

Something was moving toward him.

Something long forgotten yet never lost.

Something he had been waiting for his entire life without knowing it.

He exhaled shakily, eyes glistening.

Tonight was different.

He could feel it.

The world felt thinner, as if two distant lives were drifting closer, reaching for one another through the dark.

George closed his eyes.

Far away, Samuel did the same.

Two boys.

Two heartbeats.

Two halves of a story that had been split apart before they could understand a single page of it.

And on this quiet night, under the same moon and hidden sky, their lives trembled on the edge of reunion.

The night held its breath.

Something had begun.

Chapter Ten

◆

Sarah's Confession

The first light of dawn crept quietly into Samuel's bedroom, pale and hesitant, as though unsure whether it had permission to enter. It painted a faint glow along the edges of his desk, touched the corner of his bookshelf, and settled softly across his quilt. Even before his eyes opened, Samuel sensed the change in the air.

He awoke not with a sudden gasp, but with a slow, steady inhale, as if rising gently from beneath deep water. For a moment he lay motionless beneath the blanket. His breathing was calm, his vision unfocused, yet his heartbeat was loud and clear in his ears.

Not loud because it was fast.

Not loud because it was weak.

Loud because it did not feel like his alone.

He opened his eyes fully and stared at the ceiling. The familiar cracks and lines in the plaster greeted him, unchanged from yesterday and every day before it. Yet something inside him was undeniably different.

The feeling from the night had not faded with sleep.

It lingered.

Persistent.

Alive.

A faint trembling sensation rested beneath his ribs, pulsing gently like another presence leaning against his heart. He lifted a hand and pressed his palm to his chest.

There it was.

The unmistakable rhythm.

Steady.

Calm.

Shared.

He sat up slowly, letting the blanket slide off his shoulders. Cool air touched his skin, sending a shiver down his spine. He rubbed his arms instinctively before swinging his legs over the edge of the bed.

Every morning before this one had felt predictable.

He woke.

He prepared.

He functioned.

But this morning carried a quiet urgency. A sense that something significant had begun to shift beneath the surface of his orderly life.

His room was still and silent. His books were arranged neatly on their shelves. His school uniform hung perfectly on the chair where he had placed it last night. Everything was just as he had left it.

Only he was not the same.

He stood and walked toward the window. Outside, mist curled gently along the rooftops, thin and ghostlike, drifting through the early morning chill. The sun had not yet climbed above the buildings, but the sky was brightening by degrees.

He leaned closer to the glass, exhaling softly. The warmth of his breath fogged a small circle on the surface. Somewhere beyond the mist and the rooftops, beyond the quiet streets stretching into the distance, he felt something pulling him.

Calling him.

His fingers curled slightly against the window frame.

He turned to look at his desk.

The postcard lay where he had left it. The pale light washed over it, illuminating the faded photograph of the small seaside town. The water in the picture was calm. The sky a pale shade of blue. And at the edge of the town stood the lighthouse, tall and solitary.

Samuel reached for it.

The moment his fingers touched the worn

cardboard, a quiet jolt ran through him, soft but firm, like a whisper brushing directly against his heart.

He traced the lighthouse again.

Why did it feel familiar.

Why did it feel like an echo of a place he had once known.

Or a place he had been meant to know.

A sudden knock shook his attention back into the room.

His father's voice drifted through the door. "Sam. Breakfast in a few minutes."

Samuel swallowed, pushing his unsettled feelings down. "I will be there."

When he glanced at the mirror, he saw the usual boy staring back at him.

The neat hair.

The steady eyes.

The composed expression.

Yet beneath that familiar exterior, a deeper tension stirred. Something restless and urgent.

He dressed carefully, each motion practiced, though his fingers moved quicker than usual. It was as if his body already knew that today would not be like other days.

Across the city
in another room warmed by morning light
George woke with a sudden breath.

The hospital room was bright, radiant in a way it had not been in a long time. Sunlight streamed through the window, creating delicate patterns on the floor and the blankets. Dust motes floated lazily in the glow, dancing gently in the stillness.

George blinked, then blinked again, adjusting to the brightness.

His body ached, but the ache felt distant today, softened by something else moving gently through him. Something warm.

He turned his head.

His mother was still asleep, her cheek resting against the edge of the mattress, her hair falling loosely over her shoulder. Her hand was on his arm, as though she had held on through the night, unwilling to drift too far even in her dreams.

George's heart softened at the sight.

He did not want to disturb her.

He let his gaze drift toward the sunlight instead.

Something stirred inside him.

Not pain.

Not fear.

Not the weariness that clung to him most days.

A different feeling.

A steady, quiet thrum beneath his ribs.

He pressed a hand to his chest.

The rhythm was there.

Clear.

Gentle.

And not entirely his.

His breath trembled.

The sensation felt impossibly familiar, like a memory he had never made but somehow remembered with startling clarity. It was the same pulse from the night before. The same presence he felt reaching toward him through darkness.

He whispered, "You are out there."

The words drifted into the light and dissolved.

A breeze stirred the curtain.

He glanced at the window. The sky was a soft blue, the kind that promised a warm day, and for the first time in a long time, George felt the longing to be outside. To breathe real air. To feel sunlight on his face, not filtered through glass.

He swallowed, gathering a small courage he did not know he still had.

"Can we open the window," he asked quietly when his mother finally stirred.

Sarah blinked awake in surprise. "The window? It is chilly this morning."

"I want to feel the air."

She hesitated, then nodded. She stood, walked to the window, and pushed it open just a little.

Cold morning air slipped into the room.

George inhaled.

Salt.

Wind.

A hint of sea.

His eyes widened.

He had smelled this before.

He was certain.

Even if he could not name when or where.

He closed his eyes again.

A single truth pulsed through him.

Soft but certain.

Fragile but unshakable.

Something was coming.

Something he had waited for without understanding what he was waiting for.

His heart beat again, steady and sure, like a signal meeting its answer.

Meanwhile, at school, Samuel stood at the gate long after the bell rang.

Students rushed past him, laughing, talking, carrying their lunches, bumping shoulders playfully. The ordinary chaos of school life swirled all around him.

But Samuel was quiet.

Still.

The postcard sat safely in his pocket, its edges warm against his fingertips. The lighthouse felt like an anchor and a promise at once.

He looked toward the sky, his breath calm.

A truth had begun forming inside him.

Small at first.

Now undeniable.

He needed answers.

No more avoiding the questions.

No more pretending not to notice the missing piece of his life.

No more silence.

Tonight, he would confront his father.

Tonight, he would demand the truth.

The distance between the two boys — though wide in miles — was already shrinking.

Something ancient,

something hidden,

something powerful,

had awakened in both their hearts.

Morning had only begun,

but the story that had slept for twelve years was finally opening its eyes.

Chapter Eleven

◆

The First Contact

Samuel's heart was pounding with such force that he wondered if the sound might echo through the kitchen walls. The room around him was still, almost unnaturally so, as if the world itself had paused to watch this moment unfold. He sat rigidly at the kitchen table, pushing aside a half eaten sandwich that he had long forgotten about. His appetite had vanished the instant he saw the envelope.

The envelope lay in front of him like a living thing, as if it were breathing in the quiet. It was small, almost delicate, but to Samuel it felt impossibly heavy. The neat handwriting across the front of it made his stomach twist. He recognized the name without needing to read it twice. It vibrated through him, filling his ribs and settling deep into the space that had always felt empty.

A delivery man had handed it over minutes earlier, unaware of the storm it carried. He had given a casual nod and a faint smile before walking down the driveway, leaving Samuel rooted in place. Samuel had stood there for several seconds, staring down at the letter, unable to move, unable to speak, barely able to breathe.

He knew.

He knew the moment he saw the return address.

This letter was from George.

That hollow ache he had lived with for years surged upward, tugging at something inside him that had never been given a name until now. It was no longer a vague emptiness. It belonged to someone. Someone with a face. A voice. A life. Someone who should have grown up beside him. Someone who shared his blood.

Someone who shared his heartbeat.

With trembling fingers, Samuel reached for the envelope. The sound of paper tearing felt deafening in the silence. He opened it carefully, almost reverently, as if the slightest mishandling would cause the entire moment to shatter like glass.

Inside, there was a single sheet of paper folded in half. The page felt fragile and worn, as though it had been held too tightly by someone else before making the journey here. Samuel hesitated before unfolding it, inhaling deeply, steadying the trembling in his hands.

Then he opened it.

And the moment he began reading, it felt as if the world around him tilted. His breath hitched. His eyes moved slowly, tracing every word as if they were threads that pulled directly at his chest.

The words were simple.

But they changed everything.

Samuel,

I know that we have online contacts, but it has been harder to access my phone throughout these surgeries. I am not sure how to start this. I am writing because I have been looking for you for as long as I can remember. I found you through some old social media posts, hospital records, anything I could get my hands on. I know this might seem out of the blue, but I could not wait any longer to reach out. I have been keeping this inside for so long, and now that I have found you, I feel like I am finally able to breathe again.

Samuel blinked rapidly as his vision blurred at the edges. He set the paper down briefly, pressing his thumb against his eyelid until the spinning settled. He forced himself to keep reading.

There is so much I want to say. So much I have been carrying around. First, I need you to know something important. I am sick. Really sick. I have been in and out of hospitals for years now. I am tired, Samuel. Tired of fighting and tired of being alone. Mum has always been there for me, but I have always felt like something was missing. Like there is a part of me that is just not complete.

I do not know why we were kept apart. I do not know the reason for any of this, but I do know one thing. I need to meet you. I need to see you. I need to know my twin. Before it is too late.

I do not want you to feel pressured. I know you probably have questions and fears and concerns. I respect that. But please, Samuel, I am asking you. Let us meet. I want to know you. I want to know the brother I never had the chance to grow up with.

I hope you will want the same thing.

With all my heart,

George

The letter slipped from Samuel's fingers and drifted lightly onto the table. He sank back into his chair, the air around him seeming to change temperature. For a moment, he could not hear anything. Not the ticking of the clock. Not the hum of the refrigerator. Not the faint sound of traffic outside.

Only his heartbeat.

The words of the letter echoed inside him, repeating themselves, louder each time. George was sick. Not just unwell. Sick enough to spend years in hospitals, sick enough to write words that trembled with urgency.

His twin brother was fighting something Samuel had never even known existed.

A wave of nausea rolled through him. His breathing grew shallow. He pressed a trembling hand to his forehead, trying to slow the spinning world around him.

He had not known.

He had not even known that George existed until recently.

And now this.

The ache inside him, the one he had grown so accustomed to that he hardly noticed it anymore, suddenly sharpened into something painful. Something real. As if the emptiness was finally showing its true shape.

A hollow space that had always belonged to George.

Samuel's breath caught. The guilt clawed at him, cold and biting. George had been suffering alone. He had been carrying something heavy while Samuel lived his life without the faintest idea that his other half was out there somewhere, struggling in a hospital bed.

His mind swirled with questions he had no answers to. How could their parents do this. How could they hide something this monumental. How could Samuel go so long without sensing that someone important had been missing from his life.

He closed his eyes, inhaling shakily as the panic rose. He imagined George. Pale. Fragile. Fighting. He imagined the loneliness in George's words, the exhaustion behind them, the desperation of someone who had reached the edge of his strength.

Then he opened his eyes again.

And something inside him shifted.

He stood so abruptly that his chair scratched against

the tiles. He paced the kitchen in quick steps, gripping the letter so tightly that the edges dug into his fingers. His breath grew faster with each passing second.

Fear swirled inside him.

So did confusion.

And yet beneath all of it, there was something stronger.

Something fierce.

Something determined.

He stopped pacing and pressed both hands flat on the table, leaning over the letter, reading the final lines again.

I need to know my twin. Before it is too late.

The words wrapped themselves around him, not as a plea, but as a lifeline. George was reaching out not only for connection, but for time. For a chance. For someone who had been missing from his life since the day he was born.

Samuel swallowed hard.

He could not turn away.

Not now.

Not ever.

He stared down at the letter, letting his breath settle.

"Yes," he whispered into the quiet kitchen. "I will meet you."

His voice shook, but the truth in it was steady.

The letter had been the first contact.

The first bridge between two lives that had grown separately but were never meant to remain apart.

Samuel did not know what the future held. He did not know what would happen when they met, what answers they would find, or what pain they might uncover.

But one thing was certain.

George would not face his battle alone.

Not anymore.

And for the first time in Samuel's life, the empty space inside his chest felt as if it might finally begin to mend.

Chapter Twelve

◆

Emotional Turmoil

The house was silent, wrapped in a blanket of stillness that made every sound magnify. Samuel sat on the edge of his bed, his fingers curled loosely against the sheets as he tried to steady his breathing. The room around him was dark, the curtains drawn, leaving only the faint glow of a distant streetlamp seeping through the fabric. Shadows clung to the corners of the room, watching him, echoing the chaos inside him.

The weight of the past few days pressed heavily on his chest. It felt almost physical, as though something enormous sat against his ribs, refusing to move. Every hour seemed to bring another wave of memories, questions and emotions that tangled together until he could no longer tell where one feeling ended and another began.

The documents had shattered his world. Cold papers filled with medical notes, dates, signatures and explanations that were never meant for him. Papers that told him everything he had not known. Papers that revealed everything he had been denied. A twin. A brother. A life that had always been intertwined with his, yet carefully hidden away.

He could not look at those documents again without feeling the ground tilt beneath him.

He leaned forward slowly, resting his elbows on his knees, and let his head fall into his hands. The movement felt heavy, as if the simple act of lowering his head required strength he no longer had. His breath came out unevenly.

George.

His twin.

The boy who shared his blood.

The boy who shared something deeper than blood, something he did not yet have a name for.

Samuel squeezed his eyes shut. The room spun around him. He had grown up believing he was alone, believing he was the only child in a quiet two person household. He had built routines, expectations and dreams based on that belief. And then, within days, everything changed. The silent truth that had existed beneath his life all this time now felt loud, bright and impossible to avoid.

He had to meet George.

He knew that.

He felt it deep inside him, in the place where the strange tug had lived for years.

But the more he thought about meeting him, the more uncertain he became.

He lifted his head and stared at the wall in front of him, though he could barely see it through the darkness. Anger rose inside him slowly, like a flame licking upward in a quiet room.

Why.

Why had they hidden this.

Why had his father kept this enormous truth from him.

His jaw tightened as the conversation replayed in his head. Jack's tired expression, the halting explanations, the apologies that came too late to matter. Samuel could still hear his father's voice saying things meant to soothe him, but nothing had soothed him. Everything had felt like an excuse. Everything had felt like an attempt to cover decisions that could not be repaired.

You did not think I could handle it.

Samuel could still hear himself saying the words, sharp with disbelief and raw emotion.

Now, though, those words echoed back to him with a different tone. They sounded as though they belonged to someone else, someone younger, someone who still believed adults always made the right choices. They were hollow now, brittle with disappointment.

His father had not kept the truth because he believed it was right. He had kept it because he was afraid. Afraid of consequences. Afraid of reliving the past. Afraid of losing the fragile stability he thought he had built.

Samuel ran both hands through his hair, gripping the strands tightly as he tried to push away the sudden burn behind his eyes.

Samuel deserved to know.

He had deserved to grow up knowing he had a brother.

He had deserved to know that half of him was somewhere else in the world.

The betrayal settled deep in his bones, heavy and cold. He had always tried to be the strong one, the reliable one, the one who did not break under pressure. But now he felt cracked down the center. Everything he had believed about his life had been shifted. Tilted. Replaced by a truth too large to fit into the space where the lie had been.

His heart constricted painfully as his thoughts turned to George.

Images he had never seen began to form in his mind. A boy lying in a hospital bed, thin from all the treatments. A boy whose fingers trembled when he tried to write. A boy who stared out windows because he could not join the world beyond them. A boy who had fought battles Samuel could not even imagine.

George.

His twin.

His other half.

Sick and alone.

Samuel felt the guilt wash through him like a tide that threatened to pull him underwater. He had been oblivious. He had been living quietly, moving through routines, going to school, eating breakfast, walking through hallways without knowing that someone else was fighting for breath in a hospital room.

He stood up abruptly. His chest was too tight to remain still. He paced the length of his room, each step uneven, his hands tightening and loosening at his sides. Anger and sadness twisted around each other until he could no longer separate what belonged to which emotion.

He could not decide which hurt more.

The anger at his father.

Or the sadness for George.

Both feelings pressed on him from opposite sides, tearing at him. One felt sharp and immediate, stabbing through his thoughts. The other felt slow and steady, like a hand around his throat that refused to let go.

But there was another emotion.

A quieter one.

A colder one.

Fear.

Samuel stopped pacing and turned toward the window, staring at the night sky beyond the glass. The darkness outside was deep and endless, and it mirrored how he felt inside.

Meeting George terrified him.

What if George did not want him.

What if the bond between them had been destroyed long before now.

What if the years apart had created a distance that could never be crossed.

What if Samuel was not enough.

What if George saw him and felt nothing.

He swallowed hard.

He pictured walking into a hospital room and seeing George for the first time. He could already imagine the machines, the quiet beeping, the sterile scent of disinfectant, the shadows beneath George's eyes. He could imagine George turning toward him with hope, fear or disappointment.

His knees felt unsteady.

He returned to the bed and sank down slowly, his hands trembling as he supported his weight. Exhaustion flooded through his body like a second pulse.

He had always prided himself on being able to handle anything, on keeping his emotions locked neatly within walls he had built over years. But those walls were crumbling now.

He pressed both hands over his face.

How could he ever be ready for this.

How could he face George when he could barely face the truth of his own life.

How could he walk into that room and see himself reflected in a boy who had suffered so much.

His thoughts spiraled again.

His father had said George might not be ready.

But what if Samuel was the one who was not ready.

What if neither of them were.

Samuel lowered his hands and stared at the floor, letting out a slow breath that trembled as it left him.

He wanted to know George.

He needed to know him.

But every fear, every doubt, every question still wrapped itself around his ribs like vines that refused to loosen their grip.

He closed his eyes again.

George.

The name pulsed in his mind, warm and steady.

The invisible thread between them tugged gently.

No matter how afraid he was, the pull was there.

Constant.

Quiet.

Unyielding.

Despite the confusion and anger, despite the grief and fear, a small voice inside him whispered that he had to move forward. He had to face the truth. He had to face George.

Because that thread tying them together had existed long before Samuel ever knew it.

And now that he did know, he could not run from it.

Not anymore.

The truth had surfaced.

The secret had been broken open.

The path ahead was terrifying and uncertain.

But George was waiting.

And Samuel understood, with a clarity that surprised him, that some answers could only be found when he walked toward the person who shared his beginning.

No matter how scared he was, he would have to take the first step.

Because the future waited.

And so did George.

Chapter Thirteen

◆

George's Decision

The afternoon sun filtered weakly through the narrow slats of the hospital blinds, casting thin ribbons of golden light across the pale walls. The room smelled faintly of antiseptic, warm linen sheets and a soft sweetness from the flowers resting on a nearby table. The petals had begun to curl at the edges, their once bright colours dimmed from days spent absorbing quiet despair.

George sat upright in his hospital bed, though the motion drained what little strength he had left. A dull ache throbbed beneath his ribs, pulsing with every breath he drew. His hands lay limply against his lap, trembling gently in a rhythm he had grown used to ignoring.

The hospital had become a second skin, familiar yet suffocating. The beige walls, the muted drumming of machinery, the scent of plastic and medicine, the gentle clicking of monitors as they tracked each fragile heartbeat. All of it weighed heavily on him.

He knew the doctors were waiting for his decision.

He knew his mother was waiting too.

And he knew the time to choose was slipping away like sand through fingers too weak to hold it.

It felt impossible, this choice set before him.

A treatment that might extend his life.

Or time running its natural course.

Hope mixed with agony.

Life mixed with suffering.

Nothing about it felt fair.

His body was exhausted, worn thin from years of needles, tests, medications and days where standing upright felt like climbing a mountain. Every new treatment had come with promises. Some offered improvement. Others only brought new forms of pain. Each one chipped away at him until he could hardly remember what it felt like to be normal.

George's breath caught in his throat.

He could choose the treatment.

He could battle through more pain.

He could hold on a little longer.

But would he have the strength to?

Would he be himself at the end of it?

Would the extra time he earned be worth the cost of living in a haze of nausea and pain?

He closed his eyes for a moment.

Samuel.

The name alone sent a quiet surge of warmth through him. He had only recently learned of his twin, and yet it felt as though Samuel had always been there, waiting just beyond reach. The memory of the strange dream they had shared hovered vividly at the edge of his mind. In that dream, they had stood close, connected by something powerful and wordless. A bond like gravity, ancient and sure.

He had never forgotten the feeling of that moment.

He never would.

Samuel lived out there, somewhere beyond these walls, breathing the same city air, walking streets that George had long forgotten. The idea of meeting him filled George with a yearning so fierce it almost hurt.

What would Samuel look like?

Would they share the same eyes?

The same voice?

Would Samuel recognise him immediately, the same way George felt drawn to him?

There was so much he wanted to ask Samuel.

So much he wanted to share.

So much time they had lost.

Time they could never reclaim.

But time was slipping faster now.

He opened his eyes again, staring at the foot of the bed where his blanket pooled in soft folds. Each day he felt weaker. Each night he wondered how many more mornings he would wake to see. The fear coiled around him every time he tried to sleep.

If he refused the treatment, the doctors warned that he had months left.

Perhaps only weeks.

And each day would grow heavier than the one before it.

If he accepted the treatment, he might gain more time. But time earned through suffering felt different. It would be time spent tethered to machines, too exhausted to speak, too sick to move, too fragile to travel or meet someone. Even someone as important as Samuel.

"Is extra time still meaningful," he whispered to himself.

The door creaked open.

"Mum," he said softly.

Sarah stepped inside with careful footsteps, as though afraid any sudden movement might disturb the balance of the air around her son. Her eyes were shadowed by sleepless nights, yet they shone with unwavering love. She carried the weight of worry in the tilt of her shoulders, in the way she pressed her lips together before speaking.

"Yes, sweetheart," she replied, lowering herself onto the bed beside him.

Her warmth seeped through the blanket, and George leaned slightly toward her without realising it. For a moment, he savoured the comfort of her presence, the gentle familiarity of the only person who had never left his side.

But today was different.

Today he had something he needed to say.

"Mum," he began again, his voice rough and thin.

"I need to meet Samuel. I need to find a way to see him before it is too late."

Sarah's breath hitched. Her eyes softened, glistening with unshed tears.

"I know, sweetheart," she murmured. "I know how much he means to you already."

Her voice trembled slightly.

"But you are not well. You have to think about the treatment too. You cannot ignore what the doctors said."

George shook his head, his chest tightening. He felt the urgency sharpen inside him.

"I do not care about the treatment," he said, his voice rising. "I care about meeting Samuel. I need to know him. I cannot keep waiting and hoping that something will change on its own. I want to meet him while I still can."

Sarah reached out, brushing the side of his face with trembling fingers. The circles beneath her eyes deepened as she looked at him. Her love for him was clear, but so was her fear.

"George," she whispered, "you cannot make this decision without thinking about the risks. The treatment might give you more time. It might help you get stronger. Without it, we do not know how much time you have left."

He swallowed tightly, feeling the ache in his throat grow.

"What is the point of more time if I cannot live any of it," he said. "If I am trapped here, too weak to talk or move, what would be the point? I want time that matters. I want time I can use. And meeting Samuel is the only thing that matters to me now. Please. I need to see him."

A tear escaped Sarah's eye and slid down her cheek. She wiped it quickly, but another followed.

"I want you to have what you want," she said softly. "I want that more than anything. But I am afraid. I am afraid of the consequences. I am afraid of what might happen if you push yourself too far."

George lifted his hand and placed it gently over hers.

"I am afraid too," he admitted. "But I am more afraid of never meeting him. Of running out of time before I ever see his face."

Sarah looked at him with eyes full of grief and love intertwined. She had always been strong for him. She had always fought alongside him. And now she was faced with a choice she wished she could shield him from.

But she knew she could not deny him this.

She nodded slowly.

"I will help you," she whispered. "I will do everything I can to help you reach him."

George's breath shook with relief.

Sarah continued, her voice almost breaking. "But you must promise me something. Promise me you will think about your health too. Promise me you will not give up."

George nodded.

"I am not giving up," he said softly. "I just want to make sure my life means something. Meeting Samuel makes it mean something."

Sarah could not speak for a moment. She reached out and held his hand tightly, her fingers twining with his in a quiet promise.

They sat together in silence, letting the truth settle between them. The hum of the machines continued steadily, marking each second that slipped away. The moment felt sacred, fragile, suspended in time.

Finally, Sarah stood slowly, brushing her hands against her jeans as she tried to compose herself.

"I will find the information we need," she said. "I will call whoever I need to call. I will make sure we contact Samuel."

George managed a faint smile.

"Thank you, Mum."

He leaned back against his pillow when she left the room, the soft white sheets rising around him like a cloud. His mind raced with images he had never seen but longed for. Samuel's face. Samuel's smile. Samuel's voice.

It felt unreal.

It felt impossible.

Yet it also felt like the only thing he was meant to do.

He closed his eyes and allowed himself, for the first time in a long while, to imagine a future. A future where he was not alone. A future where he had someone by his side who understood him in a way no one else ever could.

Maybe, just maybe, it would not remain a dream forever.

He did not know how much time he had left.

He did not know if he would have the strength to travel or meet Samuel before his body grew too tired.

But he knew one thing with absolute certainty.

He would do everything in his power to reach his twin.

Because meeting Samuel was worth every risk.

It was worth every ounce of pain.

It was worth whatever time he had left.

And no matter the cost, he would not give up.

Not now.

Not when the other half of his life was finally within reach.

Chapter Fourteen

◆

Family Confrontation

The house was quiet in the way that made every small sound feel exaggerated. The faint ticking of the kitchen clock, the soft hum of the refrigerator, even the distant rush of cars passing by outside seemed louder than usual, as if the world itself knew something important was about to be said.

Samuel sat at the kitchen table, his chair pulled in close, his back slightly hunched. His hands were clasped tightly together, fingers twisting and untwisting in an anxious rhythm. His palms were damp, and every now and then he wiped them nervously against his jeans without even realising he was doing it.

The sun had just begun to sink below the horizon,

painting the sky outside in streaks of amber and deepening blue. Through the window, that fading light poured into the room and cast a warm golden glow over the wooden table, the sink, the cupboards, and the figure standing by the window.

Jack stood with one hand resting on the sill, his shoulders turned slightly away from Samuel. His gaze was fixed on something far beyond the glass. Perhaps the houses across the street. Perhaps the sky. Perhaps something much farther away, something only he could see. The light traced the lines on his face, the tiredness in his eyes, and the tension in the set of his jaw.

The atmosphere between them felt fragile and heavy at the same time, like a storm cloud that had gathered and stayed, full but waiting, holding all its rain until something forced it to break.

Silence stretched on and on.

Every second added another invisible layer to the distance between father and son.

Finally, Samuel could not bear it any longer.

"Dad," he said.

The word came out rough, as if it had scraped against something on its way up his throat. He cleared his voice and tried again, a little more steadily this time.

"Dad, I need to know the truth. About George. About everything."

The kitchen seemed to hold its breath.

Jack did not answer immediately. He turned from the window slowly, the light catching in his eyes. There was weariness there, but also something else. Resolve. Regret. Fear of what this conversation might do, and perhaps a faint hope that it might also begin to heal something.

He took in the sight of Samuel at the table, tense and pale, and his shoulders dropped slightly. Then he crossed the room with measured steps and pulled out the chair opposite his son. The simple sound of the chair legs scraping the floor felt strangely loud.

Jack sat down, resting his hands on the table, fingers interlaced. For a moment, he simply looked at Samuel. The moment felt almost sacred, as if they were balanced on the edge of a cliff together, about to look down at everything they had tried not to see.

"Samuel," Jack began, his voice quiet and unsteady.

"I should have told you sooner."

He paused, swallowing, and tried again.

"I know I have told you a little already, but after thinking about it, I realised that it was not enough. You deserve more than fragments. You deserve to know the whole story. You always have. But it is not a simple story. It is complicated. It is painful."

Samuel felt his heart thud heavily in his chest. His throat felt tight. For months he had been circling the truth like an animal tracking something in the dark. Now it was here in front of him. He was not sure if he was ready, but he knew he could not walk away from it.

"You can start wherever you are ready," he said quietly.

His voice trembled in spite of his efforts to keep it steady.

"But I need to hear everything, Dad. All of it. Why did you not tell me about George. Why did you hide him from me."

The words came out more forcefully at the end, his anger cutting through his fear.

Jack closed his eyes briefly as if bracing against a blow. When he opened them again, they looked older than Samuel remembered. He leaned back slightly, exhaling a long breath.

"It was not an easy decision," Jack said. "In fact, it was the hardest one I have ever made."

His eyes drifted, not completely focuse on the present, as if he were looking back at a younger version of himself and a younger version of Samuel's mother.

"Your mum and I were just two young people in love once. We thought that was enough to carry us through anything. Then life changed. More than once."

He gave a hollow little laugh that held no real humour.

"When she became pregnant, everything changed again. We thought we would become a family, that it would fix us somehow. Then we found out there was more to the story. Your situation. George's situation. It was all more complicated than we were prepared to handle."

Samuel's brow furrowed. He knew, in vague outlines, that his parents had separated. He knew that his mother had not been a constant figure in his life. But hearing his father begin to unravel all of this made those old facts feel much heavier.

"What do you mean," he asked. "What happened that made you keep him a secret from me."

Jack drew in a deeper breath and looked straight at his son.

"After your mother and I broke up, everything fell apart for a while. We were angry. We were hurt. We said things we should not have said. We did not trust each other. She was struggling with more than I knew how to help with. I had my own failures. We were not the people we needed to be for ourselves, and we were certainly not who we should have been for you and George."

He rubbed a hand over his face slowly.

"When you were born, and when George was born, we thought we could find a way. But we could not agree on anything. Not on where to live, not on how to share time, and definitely not on how to raise you both together. There were arguments. Long ones. Ugly ones."

Samuel's fingers curled more tightly together. His mind tried to picture it. Two small boys. Their parents shouting in the background. A house filled with tension instead of warmth.

"So you just split us up," Samuel said quietly. "Like we were something that could be divided."

Jack flinched at the bluntness of the words but did

not look away.

"We tried to find a solution," he said. "We truly did. But your mother could not care for both of you. She was already overwhelmed. Her situation was unstable. My job was uncertain. Money was tight. There were too many things going wrong. I wanted to take both of you, but the courts would not allow it. In the end, we had to decide something. And we chose in a way that still haunts me."

He hesitated, then continued more softly.

"She kept George. I took you."

There it was. The choice that had cut Samuel's life in two.

"We convinced ourselves that it was temporary," Jack went on. "That once everything settled, once we were more stable, once she got help, once I had things under control, we would fix it. Somehow. But time passed. And the distance between all of us only grew."

Samuel felt a wave of disbelief and hurt crash over him. He tried to keep his expression steady, but his eyes burned.

"You had a choice," Samuel said, his voice tight. "And you chose to let us grow up apart. You chose to let me live my whole life not knowing he existed."

Jack's shoulders sagged. "I told myself I was protecting you. When George started to get sick, it became even more complicated. Your mother and I stopped speaking for a while. All I heard were short updates, from other people, from documents. I saw some of it with my own eyes. It was hard to watch even for a moment, and I could leave. You would not have been able to."

He looked down at his hands, his fingers flexing slightly.

"I thought that if I kept you away from that world, away from the fear and the sickness, you would have a chance to grow up without that burden. I thought if I focused on giving you a stable life here, on your school, your goals, your future, I was doing the right thing."

He lifted his eyes again, and the regret in them was unmistakable.

"I was wrong. I see that now. You deserved to know you had a brother. You deserved to know who he was, what he was facing. I took that choice away from you."

Samuel's anger throbbed like a bruise.

All these years he had felt something was off, as if he were walking around in a life that did not quite fit. He had no vocabulary for it. Only a quiet restlessness. A sense of being incomplete. Now he knew why.

His thoughts drifted toward George again. A stranger and yet not a stranger. His twin. His other self. The boy whose childhood had been spent under fluorescent lights, not sunlight.

Had George ever woken up without pain.

Had he ever run through a park without collapsing.

Had he ever had an ordinary school day.

Did he know what it felt like to sit at a table and worry about exams instead of blood results.

The sympathy that washed over Samuel was deep and raw. His chest ached.

While Samuel had been growing up in a small but relatively steady home, with Jack making sure there was dinner on the table and books in his bag, George had been fighting for things Samuel had taken for granted. Breath. Strength. Time.

Jack's voice broke back into his thoughts.

"I thought keeping you apart might protect you," he said. "I thought if you did not see what your brother was going through, you would not feel trapped by it. But that does not mean it was right. I know that now."

Samuel swallowed hard, feeling his throat tighten.

"You do not understand, Dad," he said, his voice shaking. "I have spent my life feeling like something was missing and thinking that it was my problem. Thinking that I was the one who was wrong. I felt alone, and you let me believe I really was."

His vision blurred for a moment. He blinked quickly, refusing to let the tears fall.

Across the table, Jack's face crumpled, his own pain showing through the composed mask he had been trying to hold.

"I am sorry," Jack whispered. "I was trying to spare you from something I thought would destroy you. I did not want you to carry the weight of your brother's suffering on top of everything else. I thought you would resent me if I pulled you into it. I kept telling myself I would tell you when you were older, when I was ready, when the time was right. But there was never a right time. And I kept running from it."

Samuel let out a shaky breath. His fingers loosened slightly where they had dug into his palms.

"I do not know what to do," he admitted. "I do not

know how to handle any of this. George's illness. The years I never knew him. The fact that you made this choice for me."

Jack reached across the table, slowly, as if afraid Samuel might pull away. He set his hand gently on his son's clenched fists.

"You do not have to decide everything today," Jack said softly. "What matters now is that you know the truth. George is your brother. He wants to meet you. He needs you. But this has to be your choice. Not mine. Not your mother's. Yours."

Samuel looked down at their hands, at the familiarity of his father's calloused fingers over his own, and for a moment, the anger shifted aside enough to let something else in.

Responsibility.

Empathy.

The hint of a bridge between past and future.

He thought of George again, alone in a hospital bed, wondering whether his twin would ever come. He imagined stepping into that room one day, and imagined what it might mean for both of them. Perhaps it would hurt. Perhaps it would tear open wounds Samuel did not even know he had. But perhaps it would also stitch together something that had been torn from the start.

Maybe this was not only about confronting the past.

Maybe it was about giving the future a chance.

"I will think about it," Samuel said quietly. "I need time. I need to process all of this."

Jack nodded at once.

"Take all the time you need," he replied. "I will be here. When you are ready, we will figure it out together."

Samuel pushed his chair back slowly and stood. The room still felt heavy, but something in the air had changed. The truth had been spoken aloud. The silence was no longer full of secrets, but of choices.

As he walked toward the doorway, he paused and glanced back at his father. Jack sat at the table, elbows resting on the wood, his head bowed slightly. He looked smaller somehow, as if sharing the truth had taken apart the armour he had been wearing for years.

Samuel did not have any neat answers. There was no sudden feeling of peace or clarity. His chest was still tight, his thoughts still tangled. But under all of that, there was the faintest glimmer of something he had not felt in a long time.

Possibility

A chance to understand where he had come from.

A chance to know the brother he had been separated from.

A chance to choose differently than the adults who had chosen for him.

The future felt terrifying.

It also felt open.

And somewhere out there, in a hospital room filled with machines and soft beeping, George was waiting.

Chapter Fifteen

◆

The Meeting

The rain had been falling since morning, a steady curtain of water that blurred the world beyond the hospital windows into shifting shapes and muted colours. It drummed softly against the glass, a patient and rhythmic tapping that filled every pause in the room. Each drop seemed to echo the tension in the air, as if the sky itself understood how much this day mattered.

Inside the small hospital room, everything felt frozen in anticipation.

The sterile scent of disinfectant hung in the air, faint but ever present, layered over the softer smells of clean sheets and the wilting flowers on the bedside table. Machines hummed quietly, their lights blinking in measured patterns, tracking every fragile beat of George's heart. The walls, painted a dull and ordinary white, seemed to close in around him.

George lay half propped up in the bed, his back supported by a stack of pillows that never seemed quite comfortable enough. The thin hospital gown felt too loose on his frame, the fabric pooling around his thin shoulders and bony arms. His skin was pale, almost translucent in the dim light, and a faint sheen of fatigue clung to him like a shadow.

His eyes, however, were very much awake.

They were fixed on the clock mounted high on the wall, watching the second hand make its slow, deliberate journey around the face. Tick. Tick. Tick. Each movement felt louder than the last, as if time were drawing him closer to a moment he had waited for his entire life.

His heart was racing, almost painfully fast. Not because of the illness that had clung to him for so many years. Not because of the dizzying uncertainty of his next procedure. Today, his fear and excitement came from something entirely different.

In a matter of minutes, he would meet his twin.

Samuel.

The name pulsed in his mind with every beat of his heart.

He had whispered it to himself in the quiet moments between treatments. He had written it at the top of pages and then stared at it for minutes, tracing the

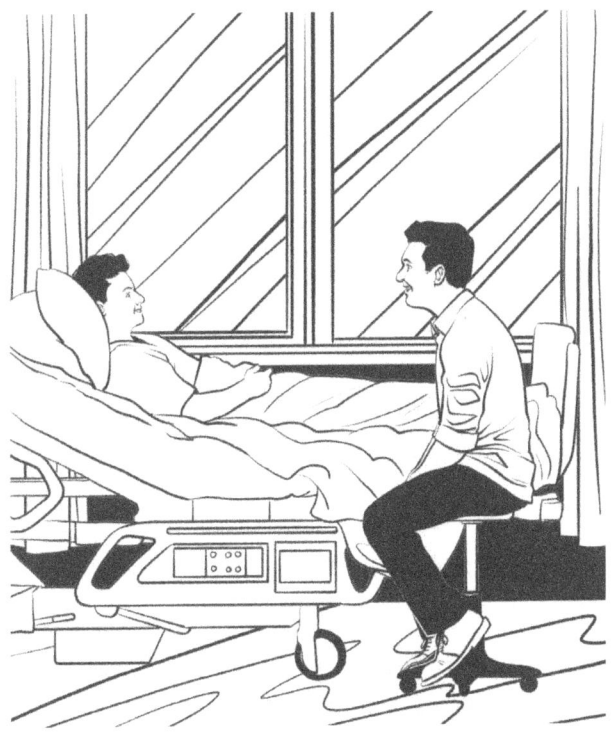

letters with his eyes as if trying to carve it into memory. Samuel. His brother. His other half. A person who had been nothing more than a shadow, then a possibility, and now, finally, a real and living presence walking somewhere in this building.

He had imagined this day countless times.

In some versions of his daydreams, he was strong and healthy, running down a hallway to meet his brother, laughing and out of breath. In others, they bumped into each other by accident in a crowded place, recognising one another instantly. Sometimes he pictured Samuel sitting with him on a beach or in a park, sharing stories about their lives, passing a ball back and forth in the grass as if they had done it a thousand times before.

Reality, he knew, would be different.

Instead of meeting him on his feet, he would greet Samuel from a hospital bed, with an IV line in his arm and monitors tracking his heart. Instead of being the kind of brother who could run or jump or chase him down a street, he was the brother struggling for breath on difficult days, the one who tired easily, the one whose life was measured in test results and medical reports.

George swallowed, feeling his throat tighten.

He remembered the letters he had written, each word chosen carefully, each sentence holding more of his heart than he had dared to show anyone else. He remembered the first phone call they had shared, his hands shaking so badly that he could barely hold the device, his voice breaking as he tried to speak to the boy who shared his name, his story and his beginning. The anticipation had built with each message exchanged, each conversation layered with awe and sorrow and hope.

All of it had led to this day.

To this moment.

To this room.

He drew in a shallow breath, trying to steady himself.

"It is just Samuel," he whispered to himself. "Just Samuel."

But he knew it was more than that.

It was not just meeting a new person.

It was meeting the missing half of his life.

A soft knock on the door sliced through the thick silence.

George jumped slightly. His heart leapt so high that for a moment he felt dizzy. He forced his gaze away from the clock and turned toward the sound. His fingers curled weakly into the blanket as he tried to keep his voice steady.

"Come in," he called, though the words came out

thin and rough.

The door opened with a quiet creak.

For a brief second, George could not breathe.

A figure stepped into the room, hesitant at first, hovering by the doorway as if unsure how far he was allowed to go. The hallway light framed him in a soft halo, making it hard to see his features clearly at first. Then the door closed gently, and the dim light inside the room revealed him more fully.

Samuel.

He was taller than George had imagined. Not towering, but clearly strong, his shoulders squared, his posture straight. His clothes were simple, but neat and carefully chosen, as if he had spent longer than usual deciding what to wear for this moment. His hair fell slightly over his forehead, damp from the rain outside, and a few droplets still clung to the fabric of his jacket.

For a heartbeat, George did not recognise him.

He saw only a stranger.

Then he saw the eyes.

The same shape, the same colour, the same way they held too much for someone their age. There was something in them, a mixture of curiosity and sorrow and a fierce, unspoken longing, that George knew instantly. It was the same feeling that had followed him all his life, reflected back at him now on another face.

A familiar jawline.

A similar curve to the mouth.

A tilt of the head that made George's chest ache.

It was like looking at a reflection of himself that had grown in a different direction.

"George," Samuel said.

His voice was soft, almost tentative, as if afraid that speaking too loudly might cause the moment to vanish. The single word trembled in the air between them.

"I cannot believe it is really you."

George's heart stuttered.

For a few seconds, he could only stare. His body had gone very still, except for the faint shaking in his hands. He had imagined this moment, rehearsed it in his mind, thought of what he would say first. But now that it was here, all the words he had planned seemed to scatter like leaves in the wind.

His chest heaved with a quiet breath.

"I cannot believe it either," he managed at last, his voice hoarse. "I have dreamed of this moment for so long."

Samuel took a small step closer, his eyes never

leaving George's face. He looked like he was trying to record every detail, as if he might wake up later and need proof that this had really happened.

"I did not know what to expect," Samuel admitted, a faint, nervous laugh escaping him. "I did not know what you would look like. What you would sound like. What kind of person you would be."

George tried to smile. His lips trembled.

"I am not much to look at right now," he said, attempting a weak joke, his hand lifting slightly toward the IV pole and the monitors. "But I am glad you are here."

Samuel's expression softened, and a real smile appeared, small but sincere.

"I am glad I am here too," he said. "I always felt like something was missing. I could not explain it. I just thought it was me. That I was the problem. Then I found out about you, and suddenly it made sense. It was not that something was wrong with me. It was that someone was missing."

The words wrapped themselves around George's heart.

The brothers fell into a silence that did not feel empty, but full. The room held all the years of separation between them, all the birthdays spent apart, all the milestones reached without the other. It held the weight of what had been stolen from them, and the fragile hope of what might still be possible.

George swallowed, feeling his eyes sting.

"I always felt it too," he said quietly. "I always knew there was something, or someone, out there. I did not have a name for it. I did not know if it was just in my head. Sometimes I thought I was imagining it. But I felt like someone else was walking through the world with a piece of me."

Samuel took another step closer, now within arm's reach of the bed.

George's hand lifted, shaking slightly. He reached out and brushed his fingertips against Samuel's forearm, lightly at first, as if afraid that if he pressed too hard, the image in front of him might vanish.

His fingers felt warm skin.

He let out a breath he had not realised he was holding.

"You are real," he whispered. "You are actually real."

Samuel's eyes shone with sudden moisture. He looked down briefly at George's hand on his arm, then back up at his face. His careful composure cracked, just a little.

"I am sorry," Samuel said.

His voice broke on the second word.

"I am so sorry, George. I am sorry I did not know about you sooner. I am sorry for all the years you were going through this alone while I was somewhere else, living my life and not even knowing you were here. I am sorry you had to carry all of this without me."

George blinked hard. His vision blurred as tears gathered at the corners of his eyes.

He did not want this moment to become an apology for something that had never been in their control. He did not want Samuel to carry a guilt that did not belong to him.

"It is not your fault," George said, forcing his voice to steady. "We did not choose any of this. We did not choose to be separated. We did not choose to live different lives. None of this was our decision, Samuel."

He breathed in slowly.

"We could not have known. We were just kids. We

were babies when it all started. It was never our fault."

Samuel's shoulders sagged slightly with relief and sorrow mixed together. He nodded, his lips pressed tightly for a moment as he tried to steady himself.

His gaze drifted over the room, taking in the reality of George's condition. The thinness of his arms. The pallor of his skin. The faint beeping of the heart monitor. The clear tubing against his hand. The tiredness in his eyes that did not belong to someone their age.

"How long," Samuel asked quietly, almost whispering. "How long have you been like this."

George hesitated.

He did not want to crush their first meeting under the full weight of his illness. But he knew Samuel deserved the truth. Hiding it would only make things harder later.

"I do not know exactly," he said. "It feels like forever. There were good days. There were times I thought maybe I would get better. There were times I almost did. Then things got worse. The doctors do not know how long I have. Without the treatment, maybe months. Maybe less. With the treatment, maybe more time. But that time might be spent feeling worse than I do now."

He paused, then met Samuel's eyes with quiet determination.

"I have always felt like I needed to meet you. Before anything else. Before any treatment or choice or outcome. I needed to see you with my own eyes. To know you were real. To know that I was not just imagining the other half of me."

The words settled heavily in the room.

Samuel's throat tightened. He took the final step closer to the bed and placed both hands gently on George's arm, his touch careful, as though George were made of glass.

"I am here now," Samuel said. "And I am not going anywhere."

The words came out firm. This time there was no tremble in them.

George's lips curved into a small, genuine smile. Tears slid freely down his cheeks now, but he did not try to hide them.

"I am glad," he whispered. "I am so glad you are here."

Samuel pulled a chair closer and sat down beside the bed, their arms still touching. For a long while, neither of them felt the need to speak. They simply existed together in that small room while the rain hammered softly against the windows, a steady accompaniment to the quiet sound of their breathing.

The storm outside had not eased. The sky remained heavy and grey, the clouds thick and unbroken. But inside the room, something was shifting.

The years of distance did not disappear. The pain of the past did not magically dissolve. There were still questions to ask, stories to share, decisions to make. The future remained uncertain, edged with fear and grief.

Yet beneath all of that, there was something new.

A bond rekindled.

A silence that no longer felt lonely.

A sense that whatever happened next, they would no longer face it as strangers.

They sat side by side while the rain continued to fall, each aware of the other's warmth, each listening to the same rhythm of the same storm. Two separate lives, finally sharing the same moment.

For the first time in their lives, they were no longer alone.

Chapter Sixteen

◆

Healing

The hospital room felt unusually still, as though the world outside had paused just long enough to acknowledge the significance of the moment unfolding within these walls. The soft hum of machines created a faint and steady backdrop, the gentle pulsation of lights reflecting against the polished linoleum floor. The air carried the familiar scent of disinfectant, yet beneath it lingered something else, something warmer and alive. Perhaps it came from the presence of the two boys reunited at last.

George rested against the pale pillows, his body fragile but his spirit far from extinguished. His skin appeared almost translucent under the fluorescent lights, but his eyes held a glow that no illness could diminish. They were the eyes of someone who had endured storms and pain and loneliness, yet still managed to cling to hope with the quiet strength of a survivor.

Samuel stepped closer to the bed, hesitant at first, as if afraid the moment might dissolve if he dared to move too quickly. His heart beat so loudly he was convinced it echoed in the small room. Standing this near to the brother he had never known, the brother whose existence had once been nothing more than a mystery buried in the shadows, felt unreal. He could barely understand the intensity of his own emotions—wonder, regret, sorrow, awe—all colliding simultaneously inside him.

"Samuel," George said, his voice thin yet warm, a faint trembling beneath the words, "it is really you."

Hearing his own name spoken by his twin for the first time sent a wave of heat through Samuel's chest. His breath caught, and for a moment, he simply stood there, overwhelmed. He had never expected his life to change so abruptly, nor had he prepared himself for the flood of recognition he felt now. It was as if something deep inside him—something that had always been restless, uncertain, incomplete—had finally settled.

He took a slow breath and stepped even closer.

"I cannot believe this," Samuel said, the emotion in his throat tightening his voice. "I have been searching for you for so long. I did not think I would ever find you."

George's lips curved in a weary smile, the edges soft with tenderness. "I know what you mean. I always felt like something was missing. Even before I knew you existed, I felt like I was not complete."

The words struck Samuel with unexpected force. His chest tightened as he imagined George struggling through years of illness, feeling the absence of something he could not identify. Samuel had grown up surrounded by family, by birthdays with candles and laughter, by holidays filled with warmth, by the comforting presence of a parent who loved him. Yet George—his twin—had spent those same years in cold hospital rooms, under the watchful eyes of doctors, enduring pain Samuel struggled even to imagine.

A wave of guilt washed over him.

"I am sorry," Samuel said suddenly, the apology spilling out before he could stop it. "I am so sorry for not being there. For not knowing."

George shook his head gently, though the effort seemed to cost him a little strength. "You do not have anything to apologize for. You did not know. You could not have."

Samuel swallowed, fighting the weight pressing down on him. It was impossible not to feel responsible, even if logic told him otherwise. He looked at George—at the way illness had thinned his hands, at the exhaustion around his eyes—and resentment swelled within him. Not toward his brother, but toward the adults who had kept them apart, toward the years that had slipped by without this connection.

"I have been angry," Samuel admitted quietly. "Angry at my father for hiding this from me. Angry at your mother for keeping us apart. Angry at everything. But at the same time, I am thankful we finally had this chance to meet. I do not know how to feel."

George listened with a calm that only someone who had lived through immense hardship could possess. His eyes softened with deep understanding, and he held Samuel's gaze with a steadiness that brought comfort.

"It is alright to feel that way," George replied, his tone gentle. "I understand. Truly, I do. But we are here now. And that is what matters most."

Samuel nodded, exhaling slowly. The anger he had carried for so many days felt heavy, but George's words soothed the sharp edges of it. He realised that clinging to resentment only robbed them of the time they had been given—time that was precious and fragile.

"You are right," Samuel said softly. "We cannot change what happened. But we can choose what comes next."

Silence lingered between them, but it was not the cold silence of strangers. It was the silence of two souls who shared a lifetime of experiences they had never spoken aloud. A silence filled with possibilities rather than pain.

After several moments, George asked in a quiet voice, "Do you ever wonder what our lives would have been like if we had grown up together?"

Samuel looked down at his hands before answering. He thought of the memories he had collected over the years: school plays, messy birthday cakes, family trips where he had laughed until his stomach hurt. He imagined George in those moments—standing beside him, running with him, laughing with him. The image was beautiful, but it carried a weight that made Samuel's chest ache.

"All the time," Samuel confessed. "There were so many things we could have done together. So many years we lost."

George nodded slowly, his eyes distant and reflective. "I think about that too. A lot. But we cannot go back. We can only move forward."

Samuel studied his brother's face, taking in the quiet strength behind those words. Despite everything George had endured, he had not allowed bitterness to harden him. He had chosen hope instead. And Samuel realized that he wanted to choose the same.

"I am scared," Samuel said softly, almost in a whisper. "I am scared that now that I have found you... I might lose you again. I do not want to lose you."

George's gaze lifted to meet his, and in that moment, Samuel saw in his twin a profound sincerity, a wisdom earned through suffering.

"You will not lose me," George said gently. "We found each other. And that is what will stay with us, no matter what happens."

The reassurance washed over Samuel like warm water. He felt a weight lift—one he had been carrying since the moment he learned George was sick. They had found each other. And whatever the future held, that truth would anchor him.

The hours passed gently as they talked. Samuel shared stories of his childhood: how he had scraped his knee on a family trip, how his father taught him to ride a bike, how he had once eaten an entire chocolate cake and denied it despite the evidence smeared across his

face. George listened with fascination, laughing quietly at the funny moments and listening intently when Samuel described the memories he had treasured most.

In return, George shared pieces of his own life. He spoke about the months spent confined to hospital rooms, the loneliness that followed him like a shadow, and the rare days when he felt well enough to forget his illness for a few precious hours. He spoke of the nurses who had become his friends, the books that had kept him company, and the quiet moments when he had imagined meeting the brother he had never known.

As the afternoon turned to evening, the conversation gradually faded into a peaceful silence. The soft glow of the bedside lamp cast gentle light over their faces. For the first time in their lives, they sat together not as strangers, but as brothers.

George's breathing had grown slower, and fatigue pulled at him. Samuel watched his twin settle against the pillows, his eyelids fluttering with exhaustion.

Samuel reached for the chair beside the bed and pulled it closer. "I am not going anywhere," he said quietly.

George opened his eyes just long enough to offer a faint smile. "I am glad," he whispered before sleep drifted over him.

As the room quieted, Samuel sat by his brother's side, letting the gentle rhythm of the machines and the soft glow of the lamp settle into him. He had come here fearing loss, fearing grief, fearing the weight of the truth.

But now, sitting beside his twin for the first time, he felt something else entirely.

He felt healing.

Not complete, not perfect, but real. A beginning rather than an ending.

Whatever came next, they would face it together.

For the first time in their lives, neither of them was alone.

Chapter Seventeen

◆

A Race Against Time

The hospital room felt colder now, even though the warm summer light filtered through the blinds and cast long, uneven stripes across the floor. It was the kind of cold that had nothing to do with the temperature. It was the cold of uncertainty, of fear, of the silent realization that time was slipping through their fingers faster than anyone wanted to admit.

George's condition had worsened rapidly over the past week. His breaths, once slow but steady, now came in fragile, uneven waves, each inhale sounding like a quiet battle that his body was fighting with everything it had left. His skin had grown paler, almost translucent, and his limbs seemed impossibly thin beneath the layers of blankets. Even his voice, once soft but lively, had been reduced to little more than a whisper.

Samuel sat in the chair beside the bed, his posture slightly hunched forward, as if leaning closer could somehow shield George from the weight of his suffering. He tried to keep his breathing steady, tried not to let his emotions spill out and drown the fragile peace that hovered between them. His hands were clasped tightly together, the knuckles white, but his gaze never once drifted away from his brother.

Strange, he thought, how this room had become their entire world.

The beeping monitors, the muted footsteps in the hallway, the distant rustling of carts being pushed along polished floors, the occasional soft voices drifting in from other rooms. All of it blended into a gentle hum, like a lullaby made of medical routine. The rest of the hospital felt so far away, as if separated by an invisible wall. In here, in this single room filled with fear and hope, nothing else mattered but George. Nothing else mattered but their bond, fragile yet fiercely alive.

"Sam..." George murmured, his voice barely audible. It trembled beneath the strain of his weakening body. "I want to thank you for being here. I know it is not easy...

having me like this."

Samuel swallowed hard. The words struck him like a blow, gentle yet devastating. He leaned forward, his eyes soft, his voice steadier than he felt inside.

"There is nowhere else I would rather be," Samuel replied. He meant it with every part of himself.

George's lips curved into a faint smile, though exhaustion tugged at the corners. "I do not know if I could have done this without you. I am glad you found me."

Samuel felt his chest tighten at those words. He had often wondered what would have happened if he had not received George's letter, or if he had ignored the instinct that told him to search. He had feared the unknown, but the thought of never meeting his twin, of missing this connection entirely, now felt unbearable.

As if the universe sensed their unspoken thoughts, the door opened gently.

Sarah stepped into the room.

Her movements were slow, careful, as though she feared making too much noise might disrupt the delicate balance of the moment. Her eyes were tired, ringed with sleepless nights and worry that had etched itself into every line of her face. Yet when she saw Samuel sitting beside George, her expression softened, almost lifting the heavy grief that clung to her shoulders.

She had been in and out of the room for days, hovering like a guardian spirit. There was a time when she had been vibrant and strong, capable of holding the world together with little more than her determination. But watching her son deteriorate this quickly had taken pieces of her with it.

"How is he?" Sarah asked quietly as she moved to the other side of George's bed. Her hand reached out almost instinctively, brushing a stray strand of hair from George's forehead with a mother's tenderness. Her touch carried a heartbreaking mixture of love, fear and helplessness.

"He is still fighting," Samuel said, his voice thick with emotion. "He has been asking about you a lot, Mum."

Sarah smiled, though her lips trembled. "I am here, George. I am always here."

She squeezed his hand gently, trying to hold herself together despite the storm raging inside her. Words felt too heavy, too fragile, too complicated. So she let her touch speak for her.

A long silence settled over the room. It was not

an empty silence, but one heavy with shared grief and unspoken fears. A silence filled with the awareness that every moment mattered more than the last.

Samuel found himself lost in thought. He had spent days living in the now, focusing on George's needs, soaking up every moment they could share. But as his twin grew weaker, his mind began to wander into the uncertain future. The questions grew louder in his head. How much time did they have left? What would happen when George could no longer fight?

He did not want to think about it. Not yet. Not when George was still here, still breathing, still looking at him with that spark of life that refused to go out.

Later that evening, the door opened again.

Jack stepped inside.

The room shifted slightly at his presence, as if the air thickened with unspoken history. He stood near the door for a moment, not moving, not speaking, simply watching George with an expression Samuel could not easily read. Jack's face was worn, his eyes shadowed, his posture tense. He looked both older and smaller somehow, as though the truth of everything that had happened was settling heavily on his shoulders.

"How is he holding up?" Jack asked, his voice low and uncertain.

Sarah did not look at him right away. She kept her gaze on George, her fingers brushing lightly against her son's arm.

"He is not good, Jack," she finally replied, her voice shaking with raw honesty. "We have lost so much time... and now this."

Jack's expression shifted. His jaw tightened, but his eyes softened in a way Samuel had rarely seen. Slowly, he stepped closer to the bed.

For a long moment, he said nothing.

He simply looked at George, as though memorizing every detail. The rise and fall of his breaths, the curve of his fingers against the blanket, the faint glimmer of exhaustion on his face. It was the look of a man who had discovered too late how precious something was. A man who had carried his own regrets for too many years.

"He is tough," Jack said at last, his voice almost breaking. "You know that. George... he has always been strong."

Samuel glanced at his father, and for the first time,

he saw something he had never fully allowed himself to see.

Guilt. Regret. And beneath both, a quiet love.

Jack had never been expressive. He had never been the kind of father who embraced easily, who spoke openly about feelings. But in this moment, Samuel could see clearly that Jack was grieving too. Grieving the lost years, the hidden truths, the decisions that had separated them all. Grieving the son he had never known and the time he would never get back.

"It is not your fault, Dad," Samuel said softly.

Jack turned to look at him.

Samuel's voice trembled, yet it carried a strength he had not possessed weeks ago. "We all did the best we could."

A flicker of emotion crossed Jack's eyes. Something fragile. Something real.

"I am sorry," Jack whispered. His voice cracked, thin and painful. "I should have been here more."

Samuel nodded slowly. There were no perfect words for a moment like this. No perfect answers. There was only acceptance of the truth.

There was no time left to fix the past.

Only the present remained.

Only George remained.

That night, the four of them stayed in the small room together. Not as strangers, not as fractured families trying to navigate years of silence, but as people finally united by something deeper than blood.

Sarah and Jack stood near each other, a silent

understanding passing between them. The choices they had made years ago hung heavily in the air, yet neither could change them now. They could only face the consequences together.

Samuel sat close to George, holding his brother's hand, speaking in soft tones about the things they would never get to do together. The dreams cut short. The memories that might have been.

George listened with tired eyes, yet a faint light remained within them. A light that said: I am not alone anymore.

A light that said: You found me.

A light that said: This is enough.

And in that room—despite the sorrow, despite the fear, despite the shrinking time—their bond became something solid, something unbreakable.

Even if it was too late to change the past,

it was not too late to love each other in the present.

Chapter Eighteen

◆

Final Days

The days became harder to distinguish from one another as George's condition continued to decline. Morning and evening blurred into the same soft grey, the same pattern of footsteps in the corridor, the same muted beeping of monitors that stitched one hour to the next. His breaths were shallow and ragged, each inhale catching faintly in his chest, each exhale sounding thinner than the last. His once strong and defiant spirit slowly diminishing did not mean it had vanished entirely; it flickered now like a candle near the end of its wick, fragile but still refusing to go out all at once.

Samuel stayed by his side, never leaving the room for more than a few minutes at a time. When he did step out, it was only to splash cold water on his face, to grab a coffee that he usually forgot to drink, or to exchange a quiet word with a nurse. He always came back quickly, as if some invisible thread tugged him toward his brother's bedside. He could not bear to be far from George, not now. Not when they had just started to understand each other, to discover inside jokes that should have been built up over years, to realise how naturally their conversations flowed, as if they had spent their whole lives side by side instead of separated by decisions they had never made.

Sometimes, Samuel would simply sit and watch George sleep. He would study the rise and fall of his chest, the slight movement of his eyelids, the way his fingers curled loosely on the sheet. Every small sign of life felt like a gift. Yet with each passing day, the fear that one of those rises and falls would be the last tangled itself around Samuel's heart and refused to let go.

Sarah, too, never left. The chair on the other side of the bed had become hers in the same way the one near the window belonged to Samuel. She spent hours by George's bed, talking to him in soft, loving tones even when his eyes were closed and his responses were little more than faint murmurs. She told him stories about his childhood, filling in the gaps he had never been able to remember clearly. She spoke about the way he used to grip her finger as a baby, about the first time he laughed so hard milk came out of his nose, about how determined he had always been even when he was small and sick and the world had felt too big for him.

She told him about the things he had missed, the school days he had been too ill to attend, the birthdays he had spent in hospital wards instead of blowing out candles over a cake at home. She told him about the life that had once been full of potential, before appointments and test results took over their calendar. She spoke as though she could rewind time, turn back the clock and give them the family they never got to be, as if pouring all these memories into the air might somehow stitch together the torn fabric of their past.

But as the days wore on, the reality of George's illness became undeniable. The changes in his breathing, the way his energy faded faster, the increasing quiet in his voice. The hopeful rise when a treatment seemed to help, followed by the sharp fall when it did not. There would be no rewinding. No second chances. Every day felt less like a step forward and more like a step closer to an ending they were all trying desperately to delay.

Jack, on the other hand, was quiet, withdrawing more and more as the days passed. He came to the room, but he often stood near the door at first, as if uncertain whether he had the right to move closer. His visits became shorter, his interactions less frequent. It was not that he did not care; everyone could see that he did. His eyes betrayed him. They lingered on George with an intensity that spoke of love and fear and something that looked very much like self reproach.

The weight of the past seemed to overwhelm him. The years in which he had not been there for George pressed down on his shoulders like something tangible, visible in the slump of his posture, in the way he rubbed the bridge of his nose when he thought no one was watching. The guilt of not being there for George, of not being the father he should have been, hung heavy in the air every time he entered the room. It sat between him and the bed like a shadow neither of them knew how to step through.

One afternoon, when the light outside had softened into the kind of gentle gold that made the dust in the air visible, George spoke to them all. His voice was faint but clear enough to catch their attention, cutting through the quiet like a fragile thread.

"I have been thinking about the things I missed out on," he said.

His eyes drifted slowly between his parents and Samuel. He did not look bitter. He looked thoughtful, as if he were carefully sifting through his memories and dreams, weighing them with a maturity that felt far older than his years.

"I always dreamed about travelling the world," he continued, speaking slowly to conserve his breath. "About seeing what was out there. But now... now, all I really want is to be with you all. To be here. With my family."

The words settled over them like a blessing and a wound at the same time.

Tears welled in Sarah's eyes before she could stop them, and she reached for his hand, holding it tightly in her own as if she could anchor him with her touch alone. "You have always been with us, George," she said, her voice shaking. "We have always been a family. We just... we did not know."

Her sentence hung in the air, the unsaid parts almost louder than the ones she had spoken. They did not know how much they had lost. They did not know how differently things could have been. They did not know how quickly time would run out.

Jack's face softened, the hardness that so often guarded his expression melting away. He stepped forward, drawing closer to the bed, and placed a hand gently on George's shoulder. The contact seemed hesitant at first, as if he feared he no longer deserved to touch his son, but then his fingers curled slightly, holding on.

"You are my son," Jack said. His voice was steady, but there was an unmistakable catch in it, a tiny fracture that revealed the pain beneath. "Always have been. Always will be."

For the first time in a long while, there was no more distance between them. The years of separation, the mistakes made, the broken promises and hidden truths did not vanish, but they no longer felt like walls. They felt like scars instead, marks of old wounds that had healed enough to be looked at, even if they still hurt.

They were together, holding on to whatever time they had left.

Samuel looked around the room, his gaze moving from George to his mother, then to his father, and back again. He felt the weight of everything they had been through pressing down on them all. The secrets, the anger, the confusion, the late night conversations, the hard truths spoken at last. He also felt the weight of everything they were about to face. His family, the one that had been divided for so long, was finally whole again, even if it was only for a brief time. The injustice of that reality twisted inside him, but underneath the injustice was something steadier.

Gratitude. That they had been given even this much.

George, with a final, exhausted smile, whispered, "Thank you. For being here. For being my family."

The words were barely audible, but they landed with astonishing clarity in the hearts of the three people circled around his bed.

And Samuel, holding his brother's hand tightly, whispered back, "We are always going to be here, George. You are not alone."

There was a promise in those words that went beyond the room, beyond the hospital, beyond the day itself. It was a promise that even when one of them could no longer stay, the bond between them would remain.

The morning that George passed was still.

It was the kind of quiet that feels like the world is holding its breath, as if even the sky refuses to move for a moment. The light that crept in through the blinds was soft and pale, casting a gentle glow over the blankets and the faces of those in the room. Outside, cars still passed, people still walked, trains still ran, but none of that seemed to exist for the family gathered around George's bed.

Samuel sat beside him, his brother's hand still in his own, even after the warmth had faded. He had felt the subtle change when it happened, the way George's breaths grew lighter and lighter until they stopped altogether, the way the line on the monitor flattened quietly, the way the room seemed to exhale all at once. George's face was peaceful, calm, like someone who had finally come home after a very long journey. Some of the strain that had etched itself into his features over the years had faded, leaving behind a softness that made him look younger, almost like the child he had never fully been allowed to be.

Sarah sobbed softly, her body shaking as she leaned forward, whispering words no one else could hear. They were not meant for anyone but her son. The words were broken and private, filled with a lifetime of love and apology and pride compressed into a handful of moments. Jack stood behind her, his hands clenched at his sides, his eyes glassy and distant. He looked like a man who had lost his way in a familiar place.

There were no goodbyes left to say. They had all said what mattered. They had said it in the days before, in the late night talks, in the tearful confessions, in the quiet, shared silences. They had said it in touches and in looks and in the simple act of being there.

Samuel did not cry at first. The grief came in

waves, not as a flood that crashed over him all at once, but as something hollow that spread slowly through his chest. It felt like the echo of a sound that had already faded, like the space left behind when a star goes out. He knew it was something he would carry, not just for days or months, but for the rest of his life.

But even through the ache, there was something else.

Gratitude.

George had come into his life like a storm, fast and unexpected and impossible to ignore. In what felt like a matter of weeks, he had rearranged everything inside Samuel's heart. The way Samuel saw his family. The way he understood love and sacrifice. The way he understood himself.

And just like that, he was gone.

But he had changed everything.

In the days after, Samuel moved through the house like a ghost, not because he lacked substance, but because everything around him felt unreal. He paused in all the places they had shared, the spaces that now seemed charged with memory. George's room, still carrying the faint hint of his scent, the bedsheets creased from the last time he had slept there between treatments. The porch where they had first really talked, when the world beyond had faded and only their voices had mattered. The hospital garden they had snuck out to late one night, wrapped in blankets, looking up at the stars and pretending they were just two ordinary brothers who had their whole lives in front of them.

His brother was gone.

But not gone.

His absence was everywhere. In the quiet at breakfast. In the empty chair. In the way the house no longer echoed with his cough or his laugh. And yet his presence lingered too. In the thoughts that nudged Samuel when he made choices. In the way he noticed small things he would have overlooked before. In the strange, painful, beautiful way his heart reacted whenever he heard someone say the word brother.

He carried George's journal that Sarah found and gave to him everywhere now. The leather was soft from use, the pages slightly bent, the spine worn. He kept it tucked inside his bag or under his pillow, as though losing it would mean losing George all over again. He read it in fragments, unable at first to face more than a page at a time. The handwriting sometimes shook, sometimes flowed, sometimes ran off the lines with urgency.

One entry stuck with him more than the others.

I did not get forever. But I got something better. I found my brother. And that was enough.

Those words settled in Samuel's chest and took root there, flowering into something that hurt and comforted him at the same time. They felt like a lesson

and a blessing. Like a message meant for him alone.

At the memorial, Samuel stood before the small group gathered. The crowd was not large. Family, a few friends, a nurse who had grown close to George, a teacher who had visited once and refused to forget him. The sky above them was pale, the air carrying that peculiar hush that often surrounds moments of collective grief.

His hands shook as he unfolded a note he had written, the paper creasing and smoothing between his fingers. His voice, though raw, was steady when he finally began to speak.

"My brother did not have a long life," Samuel said, each word chosen carefully. "But he had a full one. He laughed. He loved. He forgave. He did not let his pain stop him from opening his heart. And I... I am the lucky one. I got to be his brother."

He paused and lifted his eyes from the page. For a moment, everyone around him blurred, and he saw only the memory of George's face, smiling at him from that hospital bed.

"I will carry him with me," Samuel continued softly. "In every decision I make. In every act of courage. In the way I live."

Weeks later, when the intensity of everyone else's grief had begun to soften around the edges, Samuel returned to the tree where they had once sat together. It stood on a small rise overlooking a patch of grass and a stretch of sky, its branches moving gently in the breeze. They had come here before, trying to fit a lifetime into a handful of days, speaking quickly and laughing quietly, pretending they had more time than they did.

He sat beneath it again, alone this time. The bark at his back was rough and grounding. Above him, the leaves whispered softly as the wind moved through them, a sound that felt both comforting and distant.

From his pocket, he pulled a worn postcard, the edges softened and bent from being handled too often. On the back, in his handwriting, were six simple words.

He did not need to read them to remember what they said. He knew them by heart now. They had become something like a promise.

He closed his eyes. And in that stillness, he felt it.

George was not gone.

He was with him. In the way Samuel saw the world now, more attentive to small beauties and quiet bravery. In every act of kindness he chose to show, even when he was tired. In every moment of strength when he pushed himself a little further because he knew George would have if he could.

They were brothers, cut apart by time but never by bond, separated in years yet woven together by something deeper than circumstance. And even though their days together had been short, they mattered more than a lifetime.

Their story was not long.

But it was real.

And in the end, that was enough to last forever.

www.ingramcontent.com/pod-product-compliance
Lightning Source LLC
Chambersburg PA
CBHW032114090426
42743CB00007B/354